RETURN TO EDEN

A NEW LOOK AT
OLD RELATIONSHIPS — MAN,
ANIMAL AND GOD

Dean Harrison

BY
DEAN HARRISON

Published by
Out of Africa Wildlife Park®
4020 North Cherry Rd.
Camp Verde, AZ 86322

Printed in the United States of America
October 1998
First Edition

Copyright © 1998 by Dean Harrison
Library of Congress Control Number: 00-132924
Harrison, Dean, 1947
1. Animal behavior   2. Human behavior
3. Religion

Return to Eden: A New Look at Old Relationships -
Man, Animal and God
2nd Ed. P. CM.
April 2005

Return to Eden: A New Look at Old Relationships -
Man, Animal and God
3rd Ed. P. CM.
June 2009

Return to Eden: A New Look at Old Relationships -
Man, Animal and God
4th Ed. P. CM.
November 2017

ISBN 978-0-692-77817-3: U.S. $24.95/Canada $37.95

1. Harrison, Dean, 1947

This book is dedicated to God, His Angels and workers, all the animals who have shared their lives with us and to our children, Dean, Liana and Talia, and especially to Prayeri, my wife.

Acknowledgments

I thank God for the opportunity, the inspiration, the guidance and the protection required to carry out a life with wild animals. Without Him, the telling of this story would not be possible.

Thanks to Prayeri, my wife, for supporting and partnering with me in this endeavor. She has saved me from wild animals many times and has always been there no matter what the circumstances.

Many thanks to my parents, Bill and Mary Harrison, for allowing me to begin my walk on the wild side and for encouragement to write this book. Their assistance is truly appreciated.

I also thank the many others who assisted in this project along the way: Jan Giacento, who provided us with our first cats, Tom Schneider and his wife Pam, who helped us in Oregon, and Clinton Patea and the other members of the counsel of the Fort McDowell Apache–Mohave Indian Community, who allowed us to build a wild animal park on their land.

In addition, I would like to express my appreciation to all the staff and volunteers at Out of Africa Wildlife Park for their continued support of this project.

I especially appreciate the long-term assistance of Peter and Elizabeth Parkard and Bill Smaltz, who helped get the park started.

Additional thanks must be made to Rowland Sylvester for his assistance in handling various supportive situations and likewise to Kim "Kimbo" Banyan, who has, since her coming, assisted and supported us above and beyond the call of duty. And to our good friends Malai, Lindal and Merlin Green, who are always here when we need them. And, of course to T.J. and Mattie Powers, Prayeri's parents, who allow us a measure of freedom to get away as needed.

I wish also to thank Regina Ronk, who edited the original manuscripts.

And, to be sure, I wish to thank all those who have visited the park, paying for its maintenance and growth and the spreading of the word.

Table of Contents

Introduction

Since 1979, my wife and I have worked to create a companionship between man and animals. We built our house to accommodate the big cats. Lions, leopards, cougars and tigers have shared our food, our bed and our life. The animals have taught us more about ourselves, relationships and corporate strategy than we ever expected.

Often our lives have been threatened by their actions, both offensively and defensively. Our puncture wounds have healed, and despite injury we have reached compromise and a forgiveness that sustains our relationships.

Our objectives focused on coexisting with the wildest of all large land predators. To some this may seem foolish and could easily end in tragedy, but lessons learned and the satisfaction received have been worth it.

We wanted to do things in a nontraditional, noncultural way, to genuinely look from the predators' eyes as we learned from them and fulfilled their needs. We chose not to view them from our point of view, from information gained by man, but from the cats' point of view. To achieve this goal, we had to refrain from standard procedures used in circuses or zoos. There could be no whip and chair routines, and the boredom of a zoo setting had to be replaced with purpose and relationships.

My wife, Prayeri, and I wanted to know big cats on a personal basis. We set ourselves no small task, especially at the high level of predation with which we chose to work. After all, our subjects could eat us. We're on the menu. We desired harmony and peace between the animals and ourselves, and we found it.

This book was written over a five-year period, from 1993 to 1998. When we began we had a lesser understanding of the wild mind than what we came to know. The animals in the pages to follow respectfully shared their hidden nature, their values. They offered their very lives as portraits to be seen and respected by us, the dominant species.

It is up to us to harness this fight, this struggle of life, to the oneness of us all. May God bless our work toward peace and harmony through love and gratitude for each other and for God Himself. Our decisions today create the world tomorrow.

Enjoy.

In the Beginning

A big-cat circus act just finished and we were walking away when shrieks erupted around us. People in the arena area of the wildlife park ran in panic toward the nearest building, crowding through the restroom doors. On the edge of the melee, my wife, Prayeri, and I felt a wave of hysteria wash over us. Knowing Prayeri would be safe in that location, I turned around and headed in the direction of the screams and commotion.

I jumped over a chain-link fence, hardly noticing the obstacle and barely aware of the ground when I landed. I looked up to see the largest of the show's tigers running across the park, about a hundred feet ahead. He looked huge, at least six hundred pounds, and was traveling fast. His jaws clinched around a young boy. The child's head had disappeared in the tiger's mouth, and the body swung back and forth like a rag doll. The tiger carried him into a large stand of bushes and trees.

Screams still rent the air. The boy's pregnant mother fainted on the sidewalk some distance away. Within moments, I found myself alone, the only one left. I followed the tiger to the bushes where the shrubbery grew so dense that sunlight barely penetrated. To know the toddler's condition, someone would have to go in.

My heart throbbed in my throat, and for the first time, I felt afraid. While I'd been running, I'd thought only of the boy. Now I became aware of the man-eater that lurked unseen within the screen of vegetation. I didn't want to go in, but I knew the boy would be killed if I didn't.

YOUNG DEAN HARRISON BEGAN LEARNING TO INTERPRET ANIMAL BEHAVIOR FROM HIS REPTILE FRIENDS.

Suddenly the tiger burst from the bushes and charged straight at me. Fear of death consumed me like wildfire. Helplessness permeated my soul. I jumped back, planting my feet in a wide stance so I could leap to either side if the tiger attacked me. Just outside the bushes, he stopped. He watched me for a heart-stopping moment then retreated to his cover and his prey—the boy. My pulse raced. I'd never been so alert. I felt I'd looked death in the eyes.

Overcoming my own fear by praying, I crept forward toward the path of the tiger. Leaf and shadow obscured the animal, but about twenty feet in front of me, I saw him. The tiger crouched over the boy in an eating position. His striped forelegs rested on either side of the youngster, and his massive head hung inches above the boy's face. I couldn't see clearly because of the deep shadow, but I heard the little boy call, "Mommy! Mommy!" I knew he was still alive.

Just one week before, Prayeri and I were at the home of a landscaper we planned to hire. The man had a mountain lion caged behind his house. While we visited there, he threw some store-bought chicken into the cat's enclosure. Immediately, the mountain lion pounced on the raw chicken, but he wouldn't eat it. As hungry as he appeared, my presence threatened him. He wanted his food but couldn't eat. Obviously, he thought I planned to take his food. From his perspective, why else would I stand so close, if not for the chance to steal his prey?

The owner of the cat said, "Step back so he can eat."

When I stepped back, he began crunching. The mountain lion ate everything—meat and bones.

Remembering this, I approached the tiger and the boy, still hidden in the brush. The tiger hovered over the youngster. He rumbled and growled at me, warning me to get back. It was his prey, and he was determined to eat it.

I looked around and found myself still alone with the boy and the tiger. I'd never met a tiger before. Ironically, my wife and I had been discussing owning one. But at that moment, it didn't seem like a good idea.

The boy continued crying, and the tiger glared at me, warning me to leave him to his meal. He'd caught it, and it as his to eat.

Finally, an employee of the park came with a long pole, but he didn't seem to know what to do with it. Then the trainer ran up with a fire extinguisher. He entered the back side of the thicket where the tiger held the youngster. As he shot off the fire extinguisher, white smoke filled the bushes. I couldn't see anything in front of me. Then the trainer appeared, carrying the little boy, and I yelled, "Take him to where he can get help."

LITTLE SAJA PROVES TO BE A HANDFUL FOR MUFFIN, HER CANINE FRIEND.

As they passed, I could see the youngster had been injured but couldn't tell how badly. Again I was alone with the tiger. I didn't see the park employee anywhere close and fear jangled my nerves. The great predator still hid in the bushes. Tigers are known man-eaters. Would I be the next victim? The foliage hung silent. A hush fell over the area.

Within thirty seconds the assistant trainer arrived. He walked directly to the tiger. From his pants pocket, he took a baby bottle full of milk. The tiger stretched out his neck to drink, sucking the bottle, and the handler managed to put a leash around the huge head and neck. The bottle seemed to return the tiger to a sense of everyday routine. Because the tiger no longer saw his prey, he no longer had anything to protect. With the leash already on, the tiger simply walked alongside as the assistant trainer held the other end. Together they walked to the same arena that the tiger had escaped from.

I ran to where the boy had been laid, waiting for an emergency vehicle. His right calf and skull had been bitten, but he was still alive and coherent. He spoke only Spanish. Some park staff members put the boy into the back of a pickup and drove him to the park entrance, where an ambulance finally arrived to take him to a hospital.

Prayeri and I walked around the park somewhat stunned. We noticed people in other sections buying and eating food, playing on the swings, watching the animals. Apparently, they didn't know what had happened moments before. The stark contrast unsettled us, so we left.

ALL IN A DAYS WORK

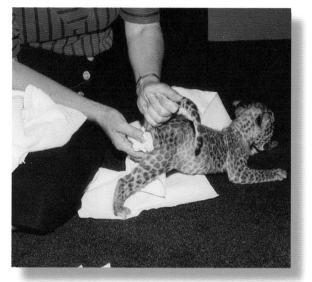

IT'S BUSINESS AS USUAL FOR PRAYERI HARRISON IN FEBRUARY 1983 AS SHE AIDS SAJA IN HER BATHROOM DUTIES. BIG CAT YOUNGSTERS MUST BE FED EVERY FOUR TO SIX HOURS, TWENTY-FOUR HOURS A DAY. SAJA PROVED TO BE NO EXCEPTION, WITH AN APPETITE TO MATCH HER LITTLE ROUND TUMMY!

We'd been talking about raising big cats and whether or not to make that commitment. In the months that followed, we decided it would be worth it. Just a small piece of knowledge about how predators behave saved a boy's life. If we could determine who these big cats were, why they act the way they do, what makes them work, perhaps we could learn to live with them, and it could be beneficial for all of us.

That was 1982. We've lived with big cats now for many years. So much has happened that cannot be explained by what I learned in school or even in our society. We've been living in a different world, a world within a world—the world of predators. We have felt their breath and slept in their beds, even raised their young, and have become friends with many of them. They have occasionally attempted to kill

CHAPTER ONE

us, and some have even risked their lives to protect us. Despite the attacks, we are still here.

We have learned their language and taught their children. They have taught us and our children. I confess that now we've become more like them than they have become like us. What used to be important seems incidental, and what appeared unimportant is now viable. Things like cars, houses and recreational equipment now have little more than functional value to us. Relationships with the big cats, discerning the reasons they do what they do, fill our lives more than when we began. Meeting the needs of another has become as important to us as meeting even our own needs.

YOUNG BRENDEL FINDS A
REFRIGERATOR IN WHICH TO ENJOY
AN AFTERNOON.

The animals have shown us their ways, which we have most certainly learned, and it has caused us embarrassment when we showed them ours, which for the most part they have not learned. The stories I am about to tell you are true as we experienced them, and their pages continue to grow here at Out of Africa Wildlife Park in Arizona, where Prayeri and I live with our predator friends.

I was born in Arizona, one of two sons to Bill and Mary Harrison. They did their best to be good parents and even indulged my interest in animals. When I was seven years old, The Lord gave me an instinct to see through the eyes of predators. That instinct has grown like a seed planted in the ground. And like the years it takes an oak to mature, that instinct has taken years to develop. It's primal, and it allows me to look from the predator's point of view. It permits communication and a sense of oneness with another, non-human individual.

Initially I worked with small, harmless reptiles then later, large ones such as giant pythons, boas and monitor lizards. I remember asking my mom if I could buy a lizard. I did my best to persuade her.

After much talk, she finally said, "I'll ask your dad." And she did.

He opposed the idea at first but by the next day had agreed.

That was the first hurdle. Now I needed to find a pet shop that sold lizards. The next weekend, we took a drive to a store that sold hundreds of reptiles of all kinds. They even had a tank filled with baby alligators, each about eight inches long.

I wanted one. A baby alligator was the best, better than any of the lizards. The lady who owned the store wanted me to have one, too. My mom was not so agreeable.

The store owner took out a little yellow and black alligator and said sweetly, "I'll show you. They're tame. I put them up to my face all the time." She held it close to her cheek. In a flash, the little guy latched onto her lower lip. Blood dribbled down her chin as she struggled to break his grip. That did it. I wasn't getting an alligator. Oh, well.

I settled for a chuckwalla, a vegetarian. These are the largest harmless lizards found in the United States. They live among large boulders in the southwest desert regions and do well in captivity if properly cared for.

My desire to be around reptiles became a fine vehicle to ride in my youth and to learn mechanical skills like building and landscaping, which were necessary for constructing enclosures and habitats. Society's vices did not overshadow my love for my friends.

Shortly after Prayeri and I met, a new arena began to emerge. We visited a zoo in Texas and had just left a jaguar enclosure. We turned back for a final look, and I heard myself say to Prayeri, "Someday you'll have one of those." Little did we comprehend that ownership of another living creature really is not possible. We know that now.

Prayeri became my wonderful and amazingly capable wife. She has been injured many times by our predator friends, but she says it's worth it. We've been learning together for many years, but with all that has happened, each year feels like three. Learning is faster from a big cat's perspective. Your life frequently depends on it.

Saja, a leopard, became our first big cat. She's beautiful. Mustard yellow is her basic color, enhanced with irregular black spots and rosettes. Her fur feels medium coarse on her back and head. On her underside, the yellow hair turns white, grows longer and feels soft. Her tail is like softly sheathed steel.

Often the underside of an animal is lighter than the top. I didn't understand why until one day I saw Saginaw, a Siberian tiger, lying on his back in the afternoon sun. He reflected the rays, and his light hair kept him cooler in the one hundred twenty-two degrees that baked the Arizona desert that day.

Saja weighs about one hundred pounds, and since we don't have cheetahs, she's the fastest cat at the park where we live. We prayed for a jaguar but received a leopard. She provided the key and was herself the door into the inner world of the predator cats.

Leopards are the most intelligent felines. Saja taught us to measure intelligence through adaptation, not association. Adaptation is long-term, generation to generation "survival of the fittest." Association is more short-term, somewhat academic and difficult to apply as an even standard. Big cats have no need nor understanding of academia. A treatise on heat conduction and air currents is just a lot of hot air when the desert is one hundred plus degrees. It's more intelligent to roll over in the shade and let your white hair do some reflecting.

The world of big cats is practical, and all is interpreted survival and relationships. Their lives aren't guaranteed, for a misinterpretation of a situation can bring an end to the interpreter. They adapt to live.

Saja excels at adaptation. She is among the best we have met. At the time of this writing, she was fifteen years old. Born at Lake Elsinore, California, she has one brother and had a sister who drowned in the rain at birth. For their safety, the breeder prevented the mother from raising the cubs. For the first month, Saja's home was an incubator. The lady who kept Saja was knowledgeable, and the baby leopard grew well. We brought her home with minimal background in big cats but full of eagerness to learn. That spotted cub filling Prayeri's arms has since led us into a new world. Looking back, we really didn't know what to expect, but we knew that whatever came would be different and exciting.

Never could we have anticipated how our lives would be transformed by just a single animal. We lived in California at the time, near Los Angeles. We resided in the country, where animals like leopards were permitted with the proper facilities and licensing. Wading through the necessary red tape proved to be an accomplishment in itself. After months of effort, Saja was legal at all levels of government. She spent most of her time in the house with us, since she was just over a month old. Her legs still wobbled with baby steps when she walked.

In the next few weeks, we noticed a major change in her motor skills and her involvement with the environment. Her baby steps became leaps. Not only could she walk, she could run and pounce. Now she loved to chase things, especially us! She would wait behind the couch until we walked by, springing out with mouth open and claws extended. This is fun for leopards. Soon she executed leaps from the top of the couch. We usually caught her in mid-flight. It's pretty cute to see a ten-pound miniature leopard jump straight at you, mouth open, baby teeth gleaming. We'd catch her in mid-leap to prevent being bitten.

As she grew, things began to change, and so did some of the furniture. We had a large enclosure built in the back yard. It included a block wall den, giant boulders half as big as a car and huge logs. Saja loved it. We acquired a chow dog we called Muffin, who became Saja's best friend. Saja would come from around one of the boulders with Muffin in pursuit. The leopard would get far enough ahead so that Muffin wouldn't see her around the rock. Then Saja would spring to the top to wait for her prey. When Muffin arrived, Saja leaped on him. He didn't like that part, but it was fun for the leopard.

Soon it became obvious: Saja needed another cat for company. She required a playmate who had her abilities. We decided on a tiger. A tiger would grow fast and be able to match our young leopard the soonest. Three months later we received a call from a friend who works with big cats. A baby female Siberian tiger became available from a private professional breeder. We made arrangements, and she was shipped from Pennsylvania to Los Angeles. We came to the airport with formula, towels, extra water, disinfectant, towelettes and a carrier. With excitement high, we arrived at the airport freight office in plenty of time.

They brought her out screeching. She hadn't eaten in several hours and apparently felt everyone should know it. Her piercing, high-pitched screams overpowered all other sounds in the building. Conversation became almost impossible.

The cub had traveled with her brother, who was going on to San Francisco. Her brother's ears were soaked with drool. She'd probably been sucking on them for most of the flight. Prayeri quickly offered her a bottle, but getting it down the screaming tiger cub wasn't so easy. People in the airport stared at us as Prayeri did her best to comfort the cub. Tigers are loud! Finally, the little tiger took a few ounces of formula. We stayed long enough to finish the paperwork, and thankfully the ride home settled the tiger down.

We named her Brendel because of her color—the black and brown combination. She grew quickly, and at five-and-a-half months we felt she could withstand the impact of play and any possible attack from the eighteen-month-old Saja. We divided the big enclosure they lived in so they could be next to each other while Brendel grew big enough to play. When introduction day arrived, I let Brendel into Saja's side.

Saja didn't see Brendel at first, and by the time she did, Brendel had jumped to the top of Saja's den. Saja attacked. Brendel fended off each tactic by standing on her haunches and boxing Saja, hitting her in the head each time. After several well-placed blows, Saja stopped. Brendel had earned Saja's respect.

Respect is important. This vital quality can only be earned in their world. With respect came immediate friendship. Within a couple of days they were playing together comfortably. Their closeness continued for about five years. They played together, ate together and slept together. They never fought, but as Brendel reached full maturity she began to play too rough.

She weighed about four hundred and fifty pounds and measured about ten feet long from nose to tail tip. Occasionally, she would stand above Saja and bat her from side to side. When we told her to stop, she did. At no time did the tiger ever hurt the leopard. Her behavior showed dominance, not intent to do harm. We've found that big cats are precision sensitive to how far their teeth and claws are penetrating and how much damage is being inflicted. Brendel was just telling Saja that she wanted to be in charge and insisted that Saja respect her wishes. We did not leave them together after that.

Ten years later, I put them together again. They greeted each other casually, showing no signs of adversarial behavior. They still respected one another.

Just after Brendel's arrival, we acquired a baby female cougar. We called her Savanna because of her tawny color. She was three weeks old and temptingly cute. Prayeri and I had gone only to look at her, but our emotions somehow ran away with us. Looking back, it may have been a mistake to get her, though she provided us with much information. Her behavior seemed scattered, and she was considerably more impulsive than Saja or Brendel. We had difficulty dealing with Savanna.

She loved Prayeri and sucked her finger but had less to do with me. I decided to make a major effort to win the cougar's affection. We let her in the house occasionally and even allowed her to sometimes sleep in our bed, which she loved. Savanna would bound up the stairs and jump on the bed—usually my side. When we came up, she wanted to play for a few minutes before going to sleep.

She liked to grab us with her mouth and squeeze, but not hard enough to break the skin or draw blood. She was only playing. She also enjoyed sprawling out, taking more than her share of the bed. I would usually slide her over so we could sleep naturally. In the morning, I often found Prayeri in one corner, curled up, and Savanna in Prayeri's place.

Savanna slept all night without waking us. She had no odor, nor was she dirty. She always kept herself clean. Petting her short, soft fur re-

LITTLE SILHOUETTE SHOWS OFF HER BEAUTIFUL SPOTS. SHE
WAS THE FIRST BLACK LEOPARD WE RAISED AND WAS SAJA'S
BEST FRIEND. SHE PASSED AWAY BEFORE THE MOVE TO
ARIZONA.

ENGLISH MASTIFF
HAMILTON AFTER A
BIG DRINK. HE GREW
UP WITH HIS BEST
FRIEND SAGINAW, A
SIBERIAN TIGER.

laxed us all just before falling asleep, and we'd wake up to a few minutes of play before starting the day. Sometimes she would lay on my face, her longer hair pressed into my mouth and nose. It tasted a little bitter, but I didn't mind. She loved being with us, and we loved being with her.

This was the closest time we ever had with her. At two-and-a-half years old, she behaved very affectionately toward both Prayeri and me. We thought our relationship with her had been sealed.

We achieved what we thought was a great union, but it didn't last. When Savanna turned four years old, something changed. We had moved to Oregon to be able to live with the cats in a "Born Free" kind of setting. We lived in the forest away from all but a few people and built a house that would accommodate both the cats and us. They could come and go at will within their enclosures and their section of the house. They impressed us with how often they came in to check on us, as though we had become their responsibility. We now know they were indeed taking care of us and also reassuring our continued close union.

Because of the county's interest and the general public's interest in our cats, we planned to open our home to visitors. Tigerville USA was about to be launched.

By this time, Savanna had adopted two cubs. They were tigers, Passage and Saginaw, both of whom had already grown considerably larger than her. One night Prayeri and I had returned home late, about 10:00 PM. The cats paced hungrily, so we prepared their food—cow parts. Prayeri put some meat in a bucket and took it in to the cats. She walked inside their habitat to feed, giving some to each cat. As usual, Savanna didn't eat until her two "cubs" ate their food. She often gave them her own, carrying it to them, and they always took it.

We left the lights off and Prayeri carried a flashlight, since the moonlight filtered dimly into the habitat. When I saw Prayeri inside, alone with the feeding cats, I had an immediate concern for her safety. It felt too dangerous. I walked in to tell her and to escort her out, little realizing that it was not her in danger but me.

Before we could leave, that look came into Savanna's eyes, that predatory gaze just before the attack. It isn't a look of play but of death. There is no mistaking the stare of attack. It's always associated with one or more of the four primal instincts: defending oneself, obtaining or protecting food, establishing or protecting territory and protecting loved ones. In this case, Savanna was protecting the food for her loved ones, the two tigers she adopted, and protecting the tigers themselves.

Fear swept through me, and I knew I would have to defend my life. I saw in slow motion, and I had the sense of not really being in my body. Perhaps it's because at that moment I didn't want to be. My arms and legs were weightless, and I had the sensation of not being burdened by my body—no pain, no distractions, no other objectives. But I did feel caught. I knew I had to escape, and I knew there would be a price. I didn't know how high it would be.

Savanna started for me around a large watering trough. She lunged toward me at head level, and I deflected her with my arms. She screamed as she hit me. To this day I can still hear that nerve-shredding sound.

She came for my throat. Again she jumped, and with my hands I grabbed her by the neck. Her fur and skin filled my fingers. Beneath the loose skin, my hands grabbed the taut muscles of her neck, solid as iron. Her mouth gaped inches from my face as I literally held her in midair. Her jaws snapped as she snarled, and the intent to kill fully manifested in her glaring eyes. She wanted me dead. All respect she had for me had vanished. Years of caring and feeding, loving and doing things together now meant nothing to her. And at that moment, I wanted this living nightmare to end.

She writhed in my hands, biting at my wrists. I held her away from me to keep her jaws from grabbing my throat and suffocating me. My arms ached with the strain. I couldn't hold her any longer and let her go. She no sooner hit the ground when she sprang at me again.

I thought if I could hold her ears instead of her neck, I could control her enough to carry her near the exit and safety. I grabbed her ears but still couldn't hold her. With the struggling weight of this big cougar in front of me, I found myself struggling on my back, and she was biting my legs. I kicked wildly, but it didn't seem to matter. I could feel her canines puncturing deep into my right leg. It felt open to the cool night air, as if a great section had been torn away. I knew she would kill me if I stayed on the ground.

Then I saw Prayeri grab Savanna's tail and pull. Somehow I scrambled to my feet and ran to the double-entry gate with the cougar chasing me. I made it to the door and had it almost closed when Savanna leaped. She caught the skin between the thumb and forefinger on my right hand, ripping it. The door flew open. She was on me again. This time in a four-by-eight-foot double-entry enclosure! I glanced behind me and yanked at the second door, but it appeared locked. She attacked, biting and snarling. Her high-pitched screams rang in my head.

Prayeri appeared. She threw herself on the big cougar, covering Savanna's face with her arm, which slid into the cougar's mouth. Savanna bit down to the bone three times, probably thinking she had me.

C H A P T E R   O N E

Again I tugged the outer gate and this time it yielded. I stepped out. Immediately, Savanna stopped her frenzy and went back to her cubs. Prayeri got up and walked out. It was over. The flashlight still beckoned from the ground inside the enclosure, but we decided to leave it.

Neither of us looked or felt the same. A substantial amount of blood darkened the ground, and it wasn't Savanna's. The heavy smell of blood hung in the air. At that point, though in considerable pain, we had to decide our next step. If we called an ambulance or went to a hospital, it would be reported. We would be on the front page of the local newspaper. We considered that the wrong kind of advertising for our newly opened Tigerville USA. Besides, the bleeding began to slow, and puncture wounds are not usually stitched anyway. We decided to handle our wounds ourselves until morning. Prayeri and I sat and laid on the front porch for a while then staggered up the stairs to our bed. Sleep came slowly. My injuries were more extensive than Prayeri's. I was full of holes. I had learned self-hypnosis years before and now applied it to my pain. It finally worked, and we both drifted to sleep.

In the morning, we found ourselves in a dried pool of blood. After cleaning our wounds, we could see what needed to be done. I called a doctor friend and got a prescription for amoxicillin. A couple who worked for us picked it up on the way in to work.

To our good fortune, a veterinary technician had just arrived to stay with them for a few days, and she planned to see the cats that day. When they reached the park, the vet tech wrapped us up so we looked reasonable. Prayeri's arm rested in a sling, and I hobbled on crutches, swathed in bandages. We joked about what the visitors to Tigerville would think when they saw us go into the habitat to present the cats to them. Their response surprised us. Everyone wanted to know if the cougar was all right. We explained, "Yes, she's fine."

I could never go in with Savanna again. If I even cracked open the gate a few inches, she grew big-eyed and crouched to attack. She wasn't playing.

In the house a curious behavior occurred. The cats had a barred section of the living room, which they could enter by either of two separate doors. They could remain downstairs or jump to some shelves and climb to a large loft. Savanna came indoors frequently, as they all did. She often flopped on the tile floor in front of one of three wrought iron gates. I would present my hand to her. She would politely take it in her mouth and put it on her side for me to pet her. This continued to be her common practice for about a year. However, if I opened any gate just a crack, she came after me, fully intent on killing me.

Prayeri also became very cautious with her, but Savanna wanted Prayeri to come in. At first Prayeri brought protection with her—Hamilton a young English mastiff. He and the cougar had experienced numerous previous standoffs. Fortunately, Hamilton always won, though he never made physical contact with Savanna. He just stared her down, and Savanna would turn and walk away. As the months passed after the attack, Prayeri finally would go in with the cougar, but their relationship never returned to its former intimacy. It always seemed too great a risk for the benefit of petting her. About a year later Savanna died. We felt sad but in a sense relieved.

She'd taken us to new heights and depths and had given us a preview of things to come, a look into the reality of the world of animals. In those early days, we were unaware of the effects of primal instincts, the principles that govern the lives of animals and how they interact with the four goals of all animal life. At that time, we only knew we had made a mistake. Now we understand animal priorities, offensive and defensive behavior and how to avoid triggering it. If we are caught, we now know how to handle it. Learning always seems to come at a price, and we have paid much for the knowledge we now share.

Java was the fourth big cat we acquired. We wanted a lion, a male lion. A friend put us in touch with the man who owned Metro, a lion sometimes used by MGM Studios. He had a three-month-old lion, Java, whom he wanted as a replacement for Metro in about five or six years. Actually, he had two cubs; the other was two months old and easy going, a cuddly little fellow with big ears. But Java was the wildest lion he'd ever seen, and he felt Java would grow too big to perform safely.

So Java became available. From the MGM Grand Hotel in Reno, we brought Java back to our home in Williams, Oregon. He was adorable and very good for almost three days. As he settled in, he began to demonstrate his lionly skills. He bit harder than the other cats. He jumped us from behind every time we turned our backs and chased us around everywhere. Of course, he considered this merely practicing his technique, and he did a lot of practicing! He became accomplished, so accomplished that after a couple months of frequent pain, many topplings and draggings, Prayeri expressed a desire not to keep him.

Sometimes I found it necessary to look beyond the moment of pain and think of a greater achievement, in this case, a relationship with a full-grown male lion who would by choice share his life with us. In all success there is always sacrifice, and at this moment we were sacrificing our bodies. All we had to do was forgive his youthful vigor.

We began buying our clothes at the Goodwill. We couldn't stop him from hurting us. The other cats never played so rough, and nothing we had yet learned could counter our African roommate's energetic behavior.

Finally, one day it happened. We put Java in with Brendel, the Siberian tiger. At that time she weighed around four hundred pounds and Java tipped the scales at a little over a hundred. When Brendel walked by, Java jumped at her from behind, biting her in the back just in front of her back legs. Brendel whirled around, roared and batted him down but controlled her power. Java crept back to his original hiding place and waited. As Brendel walked by, Java leaped and bit her in the same place again. Brendel roared and hit him, as if to say, "I told you not to do that!" But again she didn't use abusive force.

Within a minute, Java had positioned himself again. When Brendel passed by, he jumped, biting her in the back the third time. That did it!

Brendel turned. Standing on her hind legs, she swatted the young lion to the ground, descending on him with incredible speed. She grabbed him by the throat and held on. Java roared as loudly as he could, but it didn't matter. He was trapped, caught by the overwhelming power of a greater animal. In the wild, it would have meant certain death.

After about thirty seconds, Brendel released her jaws but stood towering above the lion. She began to hit him with her massive paws, back and forth, back and forth, until she satisfied herself that learning had taken place in the rebellious youngster. Then she stepped off of him. Java was a changed lion. We no longer needed to buy our clothes at the Goodwill.

THE HOME IN OREGON BEGINS TO TAKE SHAPE. DEAN COMPLETES CONSTRUCTION ON THE CATS' SECTION OF THE HOUSE.

Java was listening, willing to submit to the will of a higher authority, Brendel, who had the power of life and death and who chose to grant him life. This marked the turning point in Java's life. Thanks to Brendel, Java would later rule his own kingdom in the same way— with power under control, true meekness. He would use this discipline of self-control to teach his wives to love each other and to be tolerant when they were not.

By this time, groceries had become a sizable burden. Big cat husbandry is an expensive avocation when done properly. A dining tiger can easily consume twenty pounds of steak in one meal. Fortunately, we lived in a rural area with many farms raising cattle and sheep. Deaths and injuries were common. When the neighbors had fatalities, they called us, and we butchered often. Never once did we run out of food. The Lord always provided.

Housing became a big factor. Our feline friends deserved as much room and comfort as possible. With limited funds, we built gradually. Our land was a beautiful twenty-acre parcel with a year-round creek. We purchased it from a wonderful, caring couple, Russ and Mae Olson, who helped us get situated in Oregon. In order to properly and comfortably cohabit with the big cats, we needed to build a house that all of us could use.

We designed and built a cabin-style home for the cats and ourselves. When the temperature fell to twenty degrees outside, we could know that the cats had the choice of being comfortable. We hired a contractor to pour a foundation and complete the framing, roof, outside paneling and rough plumbing. I drew the schematics, and Prayeri and I did the electrical and all the inside finish work. It was 1,540 square feet and just right for us and our four-legged friends. We designed every room to be visible from every other room, except the bathrooms. We had two stories and an open loft. Wrought iron separated the cats' section from our section; but from their part of the house, they could always find us.

The cats had two doors in case one door became blocked by territorial claims. With two exits, the cats came and went freely. Every cat successfully used the doors the first time. They each had their own technique, and I replaced many hinges, but they always got through. All day, we heard heavy thuds hitting the swinging door. They'd hit it with their heads, and the door would smack the wall. A cat would appear. Just listening to the whack of one's head against the door made our heads ache, but the activity never seemed to bother them.

Often the cats came in to say hello, using their familiar greeting. Tigers make a sound called poofing, or chuffing, that resembles a horse blowing air through its nostrils. Poofing means, "Hello. I'm friendly. Are you friendly?" It's like a handshake. Leopards sometimes make rumbling sounds that mean the same thing. These hospitality vocalizations let us know which side of life and death we are on. They are traffic signs that let us know what is up ahead, safety or danger.

Sometimes the cats would stay for awhile. Other times, they would go right back out. Prayeri and I would look up, laugh and say, "They're just checking on us." They seemed intent on keeping tabs on our location and condition. Knowing our whereabouts gave them security and expanded their sense of personal protection and attachment.

The cats loved the accommodations and slept inside in the colder months. They always slept better inside, where noises could not disturb them.

We could see each other even from our bed. Our bedroom was a great loft, overlooking the cats' part of the house and the living room. They had a loft also, where they could be across from us at night. We found they wanted very much to be near us.

Our relationship was somewhat like a parent to a child, especially when they were young. The bond between us continues to give union, oneness, completeness, a sense of being part of something greater than oneself, a sense of purpose, of accomplishment and unselfishness. We didn't attempt to direct their lives but instead to "guide" by giving them as many opportunities as possible for play, chasing, stalking and the use of all their natural instincts both with us and with each other.

We attached large habitats to the outside of the house, which the cats used for running and practicing their predatory skills. All the cats learned to walk on a leash, some better than others—tigers are the best. We all went walking in the forest. The woods teemed with local animals such as deer and squirrels. The cats enjoyed watching them as we walked.

When we walk big cats on a leash, we con-

JAVA SHOWS DEAN WHERE TO SCRATCH, WHICH PRAYERI FINDS AMUSING.

sider it a commitment. We make leashes of horse lead rope and a chain with two latches. One end of the leash goes around the cat's neck, and the other goes around our hips. You can tell things are happening when you see the scenery speeding by. One time as we walked Savanna, the cougar, a squirrel darted across the forest floor and up a tree. Savanna wanted it and I said, "Okay."

Prayeri looked on in disbelief as Savanna and I took off. My legs strained to keep up with her as we left our current position and charted a new course. Cougars are only about two-and-a-half feet tall. I am not. Savanna confidently dove through brush and branches that a six-foot biped should avoid. We didn't get as far as she had hoped, but we got there in a hurry! The squirrel got away, but Savanna enjoyed the romp. I survived.

Life is fun with big cats, and I suppose we have enjoyed it as much as anyone. Nonetheless, I wouldn't recommend it. Our relationship with these predators has been filled with danger, pitfalls and hearsay. We should have been killed or seriously injured numerous times, but in each case we have experienced the Lord's protection. The motives for the cats' behaviors originally seemed obscure. Despite the best advice we received, we found that in reality what one thinks is true is frequently only partially true and only under certain conditions—occasionally. After many years, we can say that for us the risks have been worth the rewards. Adventure is like that, you know.

DEAN, PRAYERI AND
SIX-MONTH-OLD JAVA.
WE WERE LEARNING
THE VALUE OF GOOD
PADDING. IT'S NOT JUST
TO KEEP WARM.

STAYING IN
CONTROL IS
SOMETIMES
JUST AN
OBJECTIVE.
JAVA IS ONLY
A YEAR OLD
IN THIS
PHOTO.

The Big Move

In the summer of 1987, we received a phone call from my cousin Sheila who lives in Mesa, Arizona. Her husband, Ed, had read an article in the paper about a confiscated tiger being held at the Arizona Game and Fish Department. I called to offer my assistance.

Big cats and other restricted animals are illegal in Arizona, except for educational and exhibition purposes. Apparently a man had entered the state with a two-month old Bengal tiger. He rented a car in Texas but failed to return it. The Phoenix Police Department targeted him in connection with drug trafficking. They apprehended him in a shopping center parking lot and when they searched the vehicle found a starving baby tiger. They took her down to the station then gave her to the Game and Fish Department. When the veterinarian examined the tiger, he found her in very poor health. Without intervention, she probably had only three weeks to live. Three weeks later she was doing well under the competent care of Cindy Dougherty at the Adobe Mountain Wildlife Rehabilitation Center.

When the case went to trial, the judge ordered the tiger taken away from her owner and made the property of the State of Arizona until a suitable home could be found for her. The Adobe Mountain Wildlife Center rehabilitates native Arizona animals, so their experience with tigers was limited. They fed her well and her health returned, but the cub played so rough they felt unsure in handling her.

I suggested they follow the natural actions of tigers in the wild. The mother tiger disciplines her youngsters in a constructive manner, one that a cub can quickly understand. Their little charge bit constantly, not necessarily breaking the skin or hard enough to cause bleeding, but painful just the same. This natural practice is common among young felines. It's usually curbed with a deliberate "Stop it!" vocalization, sometimes a roar. If that doesn't bring results, then mama tiger delivers a swift swat that sometimes topples the offending youngster.

The human equivalent would be a stern, "No!" If the cub keeps biting, a controlled hand under the cub, gently knocking him over or tapping him lightly on the bridge of the nose can also produce obedience.

Reacting to the cub with uncontrolled anger would be inappropriate and could lead to retaliation by the cub. Even a three-month-old tiger, who may weigh thirty to forty pounds, can do a lot of damage if it feels that its life is threatened.

The suggestions did the trick and we talked several times for a couple of weeks. The people at the wildlife center did a wonderful job caring for their striped friend. Then Cindy called to ask if we would like Bouncer, the tiger cub who never sat still. Prayeri and I discussed it and decided to accept the center's offer. I let Cindy know we would be happy to have the little tiger if the Department felt it was appropriate. In a couple of days, we met Bouncer at the Medford airport in Oregon.

She was a beauty and very friendly. A baby tiger in a number-two dog carrier is quite a sight. Her eyes seemed large for her face and her ears and feet were big. She poofed at us immediately, indicating friendliness, so I let her out of the carrier. She promptly stepped forward, poofing as she came. In a moment, she climbed into our arms, rubbing up against us as if we were best friends. She stood on her back legs as we knelt to greet her. Her coat shone in perfect condition. She radiated beauty, orange with many black stripes and white along her belly, and appeared to be one happy little tiger. She acted and looked about three months old, but we never found out her birthday or where she was born. We changed her name to Passage, since she'd been passed around before she came to us.

We had wanted to move to Arizona ourselves a few years before but could not bring in our private collection of exotic cats. State laws prohibit private ownership of dangerous felines. We hoped Passage would be our ticket in, since we considered opening to the public. Passage's arrival triggered an opportunity to develop a relationship with the Arizona Game and Fish Department. Perhaps she would initiate passage to Arizona for us.

Prayeri and I planned to start a new business, since caring for several big cats is expensive. We needed more money to do it properly. Passage turned out to be a wonderful tiger and very helpful for our new venture, Tigerville USA.

We lived deep in the Oregon forest for the freedom to study the needs of big cats and develop a relationship with them. We sponsored the project ourselves and never applied for any grants or donations. This is obviously a high-risk project, and we didn't want to be told how to handle the cats or what to do with them by well-meaning but possibly misinformed donors. We needed freedom, not restriction.

By the time we decided to open to the public, many people had already heard about us and dropped in all too frequently. It was always pleasant but distracting. Regular days and hours for guests would better meet all our needs, so we made some signs. We graveled our quarter-mile driveway, and we painted the old outhouse. Although we lived in a very poor location for customer traffic, we took out a small twenty-five dollar ad in the local paper and waited. About two hundred people showed up. We demonstrated our relationship with the cats by going inside the habitat with them. We played, stalked, petted and overall just enjoyed their company. Stories of our adventures and the cats' interactions with each other and us made the time fly by. Everyone had fun.

That night we knew with certainty our future course. We would open a park so everyone who wanted could come and enjoy the top land predators up close and personal. But the county had another idea. They sent us a letter telling us to cease our activities because we were in violation of an ordinance.

We went to see the Josephine County planners and before long had them convinced we could benefit the community. They wanted and needed tourists, something we could attract. The county officials made us into a park, since we would be open to the public. This fine relationship with county personnel lasted as long as we remained in Oregon. They became very supportive, for which we will always be grateful. They gave all of us a chance to enjoy animals in a new and different way, a way that the animals could comfortably live in also.

Tigerville USA fulfilled our vision for the enterprise and it paid the bills. But to be truly successful, we needed a better location. We looked around the local area but couldn't find the right place. It would be another year before we found home. Meanwhile, two more cats joined us.

A call came from the Arizona Game and Fish Department. A truck driver had apparently purchased a lion cub from another truck driver and entered Arizona with his illegal passenger. He stopped in mid-state to telephone a zoo and offer the lion for sale, saying he'd be at a motel in Kingman for the night. A zoo official notified the Game and Fish Department and the police, who then met in the motel parking lot. The man hadn't identified himself, so officials didn't know which room to approach. They had no search warrant to check every room, but as they stood outside, the lioness peeked through the window of one of the rooms in plain view of the officers.

They took the young lioness to Adobe Mountain Wildlife Center and the truck driver to jail. Soon the Game and Fish Department called to offer the lioness to us, and again we accepted.

When she arrived at the Medford airport, she looked about six months old but sadly emaciated. She was the first big cat we'd seen in such poor condition, and it broke our hearts. At the time we feared she'd never fully recover. She was terribly thin. Her hip bones and ribs protruded, and scabs covered her body. One huge scab crusted her entire nose. We immediately took her to a veterinarian, a large-animal vet who did his best to diagnose and treat our big cats' ailments. When we arrived, we told him we thought the lioness had ringworm, a fungal disease which affects the skin, causing hair loss.

PRAYERI AND SAGINAW IN THE SNOW.

CHAPTER TWO

Most cases aren't serious, but it is contagious and travels quickly to animals and people.

The vet took skin scrapings and in five days called us with the report. Negative. He said the lioness simply suffered from malnutrition. So we put her with some of the other cats. In about five days, Prayeri developed a round circle on her arm, so we had her checked. Five days later, we had the results—ringworm. We all had it. All the cats, two adult dogs and their eight puppies, a couple who worked with our cats, Prayeri and I. The vet never became infected. It took four months to finally rid ourselves of the fungus.

The emaciated young lioness recovered from all her sores, and now she is exceptionally beautiful, weighing about four hundred pounds. We named her Shanta, which means peace in Sanskrit. She turned out to be one of the most remarkable cats and is Java's first wife, most favored by him. She would later take us to new experiences almost impossible to dream or imagine.

The next cat to join us was Saginaw. We needed a cub for visitors to pet, and a fluffy Siberian tiger would be perfect. A lady who seemed to know everyone in the big cat business found the right cub for us. Saginaw was born in Maine and weighed about three pounds at birth. He sparkled with cuteness. We just couldn't put him down. He loved to be around us and on top of us much of the time. What a splendid creature.

THE SITE OF WHAT WAS TO BECOME OUT OF AFRICA WILDLIFE PARK (AUGUST 1988).

His innocent face was full of life and expression. He cuddled everybody. When visitors to the park asked about petting a cub, Saginaw filled the bill. We often sat in a big circle, and he would visit everyone. He climbed into the laps of both adults and children, who would forget about the rest of the world and just love him. We all washed our hands so as not to pass germs to him, and when he came to us we let our fingers trail through his thick, soft fur. Many visitors said they considered it a privilege, a suspended moment in time.

At three months of age it became apparent that some of the adult cats, particularly Saja, the leopard, and Savanna, the cougar, wanted to mother the young tiger. They fought without hurting one another, and Saja won. She took Saginaw and raised him as her own, offering him food and protection, licking and grooming him as if he had been born to her.

After many months, Saja decreased her affections toward him, turning him over to his own recognizance. But Savanna seized the moment and took on the motherly responsibility. Saginaw had already grown larger than the cougar, but that made no difference to her. Savanna also took Passage, the Bengal tiger, and mothered the two for the next year. She fed them and groomed them, everything a cougar would do for her own cubs. Finally they became so big she couldn't manage them any longer, and she encouraged them to be on their own.

CALEB, A
COUGAR, OUR
SCOUT.

Like most big cat mothers, Savanna knew when she could do no more for her cubs. She taught them to live with others, to be respectful, loving, playful at the right time and considerate of the thoughts and feelings of friends. She instructed them to be careful of larger, more powerful animals. Life can be lost over just a scrap of food or plot of ground. Her cubs had been shown all these things, and she recognized

CHAPTER TWO

the need to let them be themselves and not a replica of her. She let them go.

About that time, we remembered Arizona, the place we talked of moving to. We made a trip to the Phoenix area with a four-month-old cougar cub named Caleb. He, too, had been given to us by the Arizona Game and Fish Department. Caleb charmed the people we met and was quite safe at that age. The Adobe Mountain Wildlife Center invited us to participate in their open house. We accepted and have participated nearly every year since.

Caleb was rescued along with his brother from some people who brought him into the state illegally. The report we received indicated the cubs had been fed about an ounce of milk per day and, at three weeks old, were starving to death. Undoubtedly, the owners had not intended to harm the little ones, but unless a person is experienced in caring for big cats, it would be hard to know how much and how often baby cougars need to eat. That information is hard to come by, and lack of food and water brings on death very quickly in cubs.

The state was notified of their presence when the owners attempted to sell the dying cubs to the next door neighbor. The neighbor telephoned the authorities and the two cats became the property of the state. Adobe Mountain Wildlife Center kept the cougars for about two months. Around-the-clock feedings were necessary every two hours for a while until the young cougars' condition improved. The Center did a wonderful job, and both cats pulled through. Caleb's brother was air-cargoed to a facility in Washington and Caleb joined us. We named him Caleb because he would act as our scout to search out our promised land—Arizona—just like Caleb did for Moses.

With our four-month-old cougar on a leash, we visited a number of potential park sites, city government offices, chambers of commerce and developers. Everywhere we went, people received us with kind interest. No appointment is necessary when you walk through the front door with a baby cougar. Everything stops, and everyone comes to see what's going on. They all asked the same question, "Why are you here?"

We explained our plan to move to a suitable location and open a wildlife park where we could demonstrate our relationship with the big cats and other animals. Wherever we went, people wanted us to locate there. Our park had the potential to be a wonderful attraction for an area.

Finally, we ended up in the city offices of Scottsdale, on the northeast side of Phoenix. A large land developer, Howard Kien, was working with the city and the Federal Bureau of Land Management to build a major tourist attraction called Horseworld. Their plans for the parcel of federal land included a zoo-type attraction, so we fit in smoothly. Howard Kien was extremely busy and his schedule always full, but when he heard what we intended to do, he met with us right away. He saw Caleb and all the pictures of Tigerville, heard about our unusual plans and he wanted us there. The physical site presented plenty of room for habitats. Water and power would be provided, and we would have immediate traffic and income.

We left Arizona excited by several possibilities for our future. In a couple of weeks, we returned to make a final decision, and we accepted How-

COUGAR SAVANNA RELAXES WITH PRAYERI AND FRIENDS JAVA AND SAJA.

ard's proposal. Everyone seemed happy. We drove back to Oregon and listed our property for sale. It sold in a few months, and we made arrangements with the new owner to rent for a month while we got things ready to move. We made a final trip to see Howard and prepare for our arrival. Everything looked good.

The same night we arrived back in Oregon to begin packing, we received a phone call from a very distressed Howard. A reporter from a local newspaper had printed an article about us, raising the fear that if we moved to Horseworld, our big cats would spook the horses. His concern had little basis in fact. Horses on a trail ride might be spooked at the surprise appearance of a wild cougar, but horses in controlled conditions aren't concerned by the mere proximity of big cats. Even zebras on the African plains graze peacefully when well-fed lions walk in their midst.

We've tested this hypothesis on many occasions in public and in private, and never have we found that our big cats scare horses. But at that point, it really didn't matter. We would have run the risk of being blamed for any potential mishaps, and Howard couldn't afford to lose the horse business. So we couldn't come.

It is rather ironic that we are now often invited to bring our cats to Horseworld (now called West World), even during their biggest horse auction of the year. We've attended, and the horses get along fine with our cats. Nothing fearful ever happens. We just draw more people to their event than they would otherwise have.

I guess all those involved discovered that horses really don't care if big cats are around in that kind of situation. Out riding with the element of surprise and potential risk, yes, a horse could be spooked. That's an entirely different level of encounter, and predator-prey survival instincts might kick in. In a crowded, noisy, distracting public encounter, things are different. The element of the wild is largely removed, and behaviors triggered by natural instincts are harder to surface if the predator feels insecure about his surroundings.

Because of the change in plans, we now had about two weeks to find another location and move all the facilities and cats, not to mention normal household items. At this point, our family included two lions, Java and Shanta; three tigers, Brendel, Passage and Saginaw; two cougars, Savanna and Caleb; one leopard, Saja; and our two English mastiffs, Nottingham and Hamilton. So back we drove to Arizona.

Prayeri had a great idea—to contact some of the various Indian tribes to see if they were interested in allowing us to live on their land for about six months. The first one said no, but the Yavapai Indians of the Ft. McDowell Indian Community said yes. We chose one of two sites on still another trip and set a telephone pole in the ground so we would have power when we arrived. We spent an afternoon purchasing a mobile home and contracted with a newly formed Arizona company to arrange electrical power and equipment so when we arrived with our Oregon acclimated cats, we'd be able to cool them in the hundred-ten degree heat. We then returned to Oregon to get everybody.

We only had a week to box and crate, hire a flat-bed truck and an air-conditioned truck and find drivers. We also needed to drive over to Bend, Oregon, about four hours northeast of Tigerville. A baby black leopard (commonly called a black panther) had just been born that we wanted to pick up before we left the state. He was owned by Dave and Dianne Hanson, private professional breeders of big cats. The leopard had been nursing from his mom for eight days. Then the Hansons pulled him to bottle feed until we could get there on the tenth day. He looked healthy, so we brought him back with us. We named him

Eclipse, which means "in the shadow of." He would replace Silhouette, the black leopard who died from a bone infection after a broken leg. She had been born the previous year to the same parents.

We loved Silhouette. The black leopard displayed remarkable affection and bristled with spunk. She and Saja, the spotted leopard, became good friends and the two played together constantly. The night she died, she climbed to the loft across from our bedroom, called to us, and gave up her spirit. Obviously, she was saying goodbye.

Silhouette had sparkled with lively vibrancy. She even played with Java, who loved her. She touched many people with her sweetness and her acrobatics, her ability to immediately be your friend. We mourned her passing. She would never experience the new park and the excitement of adventure. We still miss her.

Eclipse had to fill her paws. He, of course, had a ways to go since he only weighed three pounds and had just opened his eyes. But in the years since, he's done it. Eclipse has taught us much and truly walks in the shadow of Silhouette.

The next day, some of the people who had grown close to the cats gathered with us to disassemble the enclosures. The fencing had been

TIGER IN THE FLOWERS, BRENDEL, A SIBERIAN TIGER CUB AT TWO MONTHS.

CHAPTER TWO

constructed with moving in mind, and it came down a lot faster than it went up. As we scrambled to get Tigerville packed and loaded, just west of us a major forest fire raged out of control. Smoke covered us and burning embers swirled from the sky. Slurry bombers swooped down about a hundred feet over our heads, props thundering. We would have liked to have been anyplace else at that moment.

Tom Schneider organized the people packing our fencing and facilities onto the trucks, and his wife Pam, provided indispensable help. They had grown attached to the cats and to us. I know it must have been painful for them to see us go. As we loaded the trucks, it seemed we'd never get everything on board.

The air-conditioned truck, which measured about fifty feet long, was packed with cages for the cats and our two English mastiffs. We loaded enough panels in the first truck to enclose the cats while we built the new enclosures. The flatbed, which was equally long, contained everything else, including our household items. The flatbed didn't have a top or sides, only poles to keep everything in place.

The last day of occupancy on the property, at about 7:00 PM, the many panels on the flatbed fell off. It all had to be redone.

Fortunately, the cats remained in good control of themselves. The fire and the bustle of moving didn't seem to affect them. We freely discussed our big move in front of our cats, and I believe that on some level they understood. They demonstrated cooperative understanding considering the unnerving situation. As we worked into the night, none of them offered aggressive resistance, although Java's actions might be considered passive resistance.

By 10:00 PM all the cats were loaded except one—our male lion, Java. And he wasn't going. I asked the Lord for help, and Java finally moved into a portable cage. Then we lifted his cage in the air with a forklift. We drove him to the open side door of the air-conditioned truck and waited for him to go into the prepared enclosure with the other cats. He refused—Java would not budge.

Since he weighed well over six hundred pounds at the time, pushing him was out of the question. We talked to him, reassured him, even begged him to move into the truck. Finally, I climbed into the transport enclosure myself. I called, but he still wouldn't move. The driver got tired of waiting, so he decided to go to town with his wife and two daughters, who had come along for the adventure of transporting a van full of big cats. Hours went by, and still Java remained planted. The forklift had to be started every hour to continue to hold up the weight of the lion and the cage.

After five hours, at 3:00 AM Prayeri climbed in next to me. We stretched out and pretended to be very comfortable, inviting Java to join us. We rolled around comfortably, yawning and stretching and telling each other how enjoyable it felt to be where we were. Many times we invited Java to join us, but he remained glued to his one spot. Without sitting or lying down, he stood. He hardly looked to either side but just peered in at us. Sometimes his eyes would close, but he remained in his position. He didn't want to go. He liked his habitat, and change was not a priority. Then finally, after five hours of convincing, Java gave in. Slowly the big lion ambled into the truck. With great relief I closed the door, and we had everybody.

Our driver arrived moments before, so our truck was ready to go. The cats could not stay in cramped quarters for very long, so while the flatbed stayed, waiting for Tom to supervise reloading in the morning, we drove off. The trip took almost twenty-eight hours. Stopping only to check the cats every two hours and grab a bite for ourselves to eat, we drove straight through. Prayeri and I spelled each other at the wheel, but the truck driver managed that long day and night on his own. Despite our tiredness, the drive went smoothly.

We arrived at 8:00 AM, August 28, 1988. The mobile home we purchased stood ready, but the electricity had not been connected. About five people waited there to help us unload. One of them was Cindy Dougherty from the Game and Fish Department. She made a call to Bill Smaltz, a local contractor who had begun an organization to help bears, now called The North American Bear Society. Bill responded with about a dozen of his members, and they rescued us.

We unloaded all the cats and the temporary cages. Java was last. I had to leash walk him out of the truck to his enclosure fifty feet away. I looked at the yellow leash and the waiting lion.

It had been six months or so since our last walk together. Joined by a leash that circled his neck and my hips, Java had walked me. Where he walked, I walked. When he ran, I ran. When he stopped and rolled over several times, I knew I was in trouble. He became excited, grabbing my leg with his enormous mouth and holding me with his paws. When you're in a lion's mouth, you tend to go in the direction of the least pain. Wherever his head went, I went, too.

He let go but turned to jump up and at me, playfully swatting me with a paw. Then he bounded away. I followed in the same direction. The leash is like a commitment, you know. It kept us together. After a short jog, Java slowed down. With just a few more hefty tugs and pulls, he walked quietly back to his habitat. Greatly relieved, I didn't want to do that again.

Since then, Java had grown heavier by about a hundred pounds and moved with a king's self-assurance. Once again we would be joined by the leash, but this time we would walk in unfamiliar territory. It was Java and I in the back of the eighteen wheeler, heading out into the Arizona desert. The group of people helping us had no idea what to do if something went wrong. Suppose the lion bolted and took off into the landscape. We saw no fences. He could pull me like a hooked trout behind a motor boat. If something spooked him, I could end up in the hospital, and who knows what would happen to an escaped lion. It wouldn't be good.

We placed a three-foot-high chain-link panel twenty-four feet long down the right side of the truck ramp. That's all we had. The rest had been used to set up enclosures. Java had to walk down the ramp, turn left another thirty feet and then walk into a six-by-twelve-foot cage with Brendel, the Siberian tiger. Could he do it? I prayed that he would, but faith isn't tested until action is taken.

GOOD FRIENDS BRENDEL, SAVANNA THE COUGAR AND NOTTINGHAM.

Picking up the cotton leash, I stepped into my end and cinched it tighter than usual around my hips. I didn't want the leash sliding up or down. This was a package deal, Java and me. Next I put a large chain around Java's massive head and neck. The latch became invisible in Java's luxuriant mane. I stretched my arms to encircle his thick ruff, and I closed and checked the latch more by feel than by sight, my face pressed against his coarse black and brown hair.

My pulse jumped higher than I remembered in the past, and I took a deep breath as I straightened. "Okay, Lord. It's up to You."

"Let's go Java."

We began our descent calmly. Java walked right beside me in perfect step. As we reached the bottom of the ramp, Java turned left, following the chain-link panel. The enclosure ahead seemed hardly big enough to turn around in and already contained the five-hundred-pound tiger, Brendel. I wondered if Java would balk and turn away when he saw the cramped quarters. You can't make a lion go where he doesn't want to go. We never paused as we approached the small cage.

With huge relief on my part, Java walked straight in next to Brendel. We made it! I uncoupled the double-latched leash, stepped out and shut the door. "Thanks, Lord. We did it."

The people helping us had all hidden behind cages a safe distance away. They all came forward and approached Java. None of them had ever seen such a huge lion close enough to touch.

He welcomed them all.

Their fear of the unexpected vanished. We all felt safer, for now.

The second truck arrived the following morning, and we unloaded it as fast as we could. With the help of Bill Smaltz and members of his Bear Society, we had three enclosures ready for the big cats in only three days. Bill donated both time and materials.

Since we had no electricity, we rented generators to cool the cats. By sundown, our mobile home felt like a sauna, so we spent the nights sleeping outdoors next to our animal friends. The monsoon season blew in thunderstorms, and it seemed every other night we grabbed our sleeping bags and scurried into the hot trailer to avoid being drenched.

Electric power arrived three weeks after we did. The telephone hook-up came about the same time and water two-and-a-half years later. At first we bathed in the nearby Verde River and filled water troughs and barrels at an Indian water tank until the Phoenix Water District stopped us. Then Don Parod came into our lives.

Don was an excavator and sat as chairman of the board of directors of the Fire Department of Fountain Hills, our closest town, just two miles away. He determined that we shouldn't run out of water. He gave us an old water truck tank that held about 1,750 gallons. At the same time, we acquired a 1,500-gallon fiberglass tank. For the next two-and-a-half years, he kept both of them filled with enough water for us, the animals and our visitors, even on Saturday, Sunday and holidays.

Finally, we received permission from the Indian tribal council to have a well drilled. Records showed no success in finding water near our area, but we hit water at one hundred forty feet and drilled another hundred. The water tested extremely pure with only the high calcium con-

LITTLE SAGINAW AND PASSAGE TELL DEAN THAT CLIMBING INTO A TREE IS NO ESCAPE FROM A DETERMINED PAIR OF TIGERS.

tent common to this area. Don felt relieved, and we will always be grateful for his efforts.

Now that all the cats had a place to stay, our concern turned to the hundred-ten-degree heat. Even with shade, we baked like toasted muffins in the soaring temperatures. It would take some time to adapt. We also knew that the cats wouldn't be able to stay in such small spaces for very long, a few days at the most. We had to get busy.

We had only planned to be on the Ft. McDowell property for six months or so. We expected to find another site and a backer to help finance our undertaking, but that proved difficult. We decided to open right where we'd landed. The Indian Council proved kind and agreeable, so we signed a temporary lease for one year. With diligent effort, one paid employee and the help of volunteers, in six weeks we readied the park.

Our first day was October 15, 1988. With our proximity to the huge Phoenix metroplex, the opening turnout disappointed us with only about three hundred thirty people.

We knew we needed another cub. Our little Saginaw, now eighteen months old and weighing over three hundred pounds would be unsafe for visitors to pet. We made arrangements with a breeder in Nevada to acquire a lioness we named Sahara. She ate well and had a tendency to roll down hills. Sahara loved to ride in a little red wagon and remained petable by the public for many months. She and the black leopard, Eclipse, became best friends and remained that way until she matured at about three-and-a-half. Then Java finally accepted her into his pride, and Eclipse married Saja.

LOVE COMES IN MANY STRANGE WAYS...
HERE PRAYERI TAKES SAVANNA'S ADVICE AND ENJOYS A GOOD
AFTERNOON THUMB!

We persevered, building as rapidly as we could and advertising as much as possible. The going turned out to be harder than we expected, but we never gave up. Each year we've done better than the previous year by a healthy margin. Now people come from all over the world to see what we do at Out of Africa Wildlife Park, and each day is different. Visitors get to watch the big cats spontaneously interacting with people. The element of surprise hangs on every show, because our feline friends are free to act from their own choices. It's a chance to see the wild close-up and very personal.

We do no training, nor do we use food rewards. A relationship of love and respect between us, the animals and the Lord is our basis for interaction. We look from the animal's point of view, which most of the time affords us harmony with them.

DEAN AND BENGAL TIGER PASSAGE TAKE BOATING TO NEW DEPTHS ABOARD A JET BOAT WHILE FILMING AN EPISODE OF THE TV SERIES "MAC AND MUTLEY."

In Search of Motivation

The morning air felt hot and still, the humidity unseasonably high that spring day in 1993. I stood alone, washing Java's pond with a hose. Usually we worked as a pair inside the habitat, but at that moment Prayeri had just stepped outside the gate. The eight-year-old king lion lay about a hundred and fifty feet to the east of me. Being inside the habitat with him seemed somewhat risky because the day before he had told Shanta to come into season. Java was interested in another honeymoon. Our experience with Java told us to be cautious at such times. Under similar circumstances, he had attempted to attack us when we ventured too close, even from outside the fence. An inside encounter could be disastrous, but I thought I could complete the job and get out safely.

We raised Java from a three-month old cub. Prior to that he had been well-treated in his birthplace, the West Coast Game Park on the coast of Oregon, and during his stay at the MGM Grand Hotel in Reno, Nevada. After his rowdy years, he'd become wonderfully affectionate. Many times he assisted us in dealing with other cats, who for their own reasons played too rough with us, the fragile ones.

His two wives, Shanta and Sahara, lay some distance away, paying no attention to me as I worked. I knew that if Shanta, Java's number one wife, approached me, the king lion would take offense at my presence and attack.

Unexpectedly, Shanta came running at me. I could tell by the way she ran she planned to jump me. She came fast but meant no harm. Her eyes glinted with play, not predatory intent. She wanted to interact, not kill, but her size and speed made a friendly tussle extremely dangerous for me.

I also knew she would soon be coming into season. If she came close to me, Java's protection instinct for his wife would be activated and he would attack me. His intent would not be to kill me but to remove me from the area. However, the results could be the same.

My heart leaped into my throat as I saw Shanta charging me. I knew the sequence. If she hit me and knocked me down, Java would be on me a moment later, all six hundred pounds of him, biting and thrashing in instinctual lion fashion for dealing with a rival male. I had to do something. The exit gate stood a hundred feet away, and the thought raced through my mind, "I'm in here with a garden hose."

I squirted it at the approaching lioness and yelled, "Shanta! No! No!" but to no avail. She ran at me with a speed approaching thirty-five miles an hour, just under the attack speed for lions.

Java had already seen her take off, and I understood instantly the situation facing me. Mating is often initiated by violence, the clashing of two males for the privilege.

Even males of the pride who are otherwise close companions and willing to die for each other can become savage opponents when a lioness comes into season. They attack each other, often causing injury but rarely killing. After the conflict, the dominant male and his in-season wife honeymoon for about eight days, mating every five to fifteen minutes day and night. This often produces baby lions about three-and-a-half months later.

Java, though much larger than normal in size, has remarkable speed. He's the biggest cat at the park, and now he sped in my direction. He easily caught up with Shanta and caused her to veer to my right. Because of Java, Shanta couldn't carry out her intent to hit me, but Java

CHAPTER THREE

HOW MUCH CAN ONE REALLY HANDLE? DOES MOTIVATION MAKE A DIFFERENCE? HERE SOLOMON HAS ALREADY CAUGHT TWO BALLS AND IS ABOUT TO CATCH A THIRD.

could! The bigger lion came straight at me, his head down, his back level. His brow furrowed with the concentration of a defensive attack.

His speed was incredible, though I saw it in slow motion. The look in his eyes frothed with savage wildness—without mercy, a male lion full of fury. His eyes narrowed to a squint, the attack glare. The circumstances and body language definitely indicated protection of his mate.

I thought, "I'm caught. I can't run. I shouldn't be here. He's attacking me." I froze, helpless.

In the wild, a male lion can take down even an adult Cape buffalo by himself. I felt like a twig compared to Java.

He accelerated into a full charge. What could stop him? I yelled, "Java! No! No!" He didn't care. Only the empty pond lay between us.

As he crossed the pond, something happened that we've never seen before or since—Java slipped. His feet went out from under him, and the big lion skidded straight toward me. For a moment, the huge lion lay at my feet. I stood stunned. My destiny changed in an instant. Perhaps due to divine intervention, Java's slip saved me.

Lions are sight hunters and only attack what they see. From the new angle, his massive mane kept me out of his line of vision. He could only see Shanta, and he bounded to his feet to run toward her. Immediately, I exited the habitat and thanked the Lord. Our bodies are not designed to receive lion treatment.

This episode was one of many in which a scene in the environment triggered dangerous instincts. Instinctual behaviors require no learning and are part of the creature itself, like a leg or a foot. Each big cat has instincts unique both to its species and to itself as an individual. The lion has lion instincts. The jaguar has jaguar instincts. Some are the same and some are different. The members of a species share the majority of instincts, but no two individuals react in an identical way all the time. The instinctual package is the dangerous part of the animal, sparking instant behaviors apart from intellect.

To survive with predators, one needs to know the reasons for their behavior, what triggers their actions. I've found that big cats respond based on three areas of motivation: instinct, intellect and feelings.

Instincts are given life as the creature is formed in the mother. Both parents contribute and the offspring contain instincts that are both similar to and different from each parent, like other genetic traits. Instincts are connected to the central nervous system by the senses—sight, sound, smell, touch, taste. For general survival purposes, touch and taste are used minimally. Smell and sound are used primarily for tracking. Sight monopolizes the action.

Java saw Shanta come at me, and what he saw caused him to charge. He saw her again after he slipped, so he pursued her, not me. His instinct to mate had been automatically triggered by the sense of sight. The mating instinct joined another instinct—protection—for a combination potentially lethal to me.

Instincts are nonthinking, nonrestrictive, unlearned motivators of behavior that cannot be removed or trained out of an animal. Therefore, big cats can never be considered tame, domesticated pets. They are wild by nature. The wildness is inherent in the creature itself. Many people feel they can keep a big cat like a house cat, dog or horse. This is a major error and can produce a false sense of security.

Big cats prey on that sense of security. This is how they eat. When the young antelope puts his head down to graze and thinks all is well, the attack comes. This pseudo-safe prey behavior can be seen as vulnerability and appears in many forms. It is seen when the young wildebeest fails to acknowledge his mother's lion warnings. It is present when the physical condition of any animal is impaired, whether externally, like a broken leg, or internally, like tuberculosis. Any kind of mental deficiency, any inability to assess the environment or adapt, is risky and tends toward a shorter life. Vulnerability glows in neon when the prey is alone. A predator takes advantage when advantage can be taken. It's an instinct.

Big cats are equipped with a fine set of operating senses that fuel their instincts. Most often used is sight. Many times we notice all the cats looking in a particular direction on the hill behind us or out in the desert. Though we look, we can't even find what they see. Often we observe a big cat chasing a fly or watching very small movements of insects on the ground.

They see incredibly well in the dark, too. It affords them great advantage over us at night. Many also have light colored marks under their eyes to reflect even more light for night vision. Their eyes are in many cases larger than ours, so even more light is utilized. Overall, their ability to see us is many times our ability to see them, and they watch everything.

Their sense of hearing also gives them an advantage over us. Their ears are large dish antennas shaped to catch even the faintest sounds. We can merely whisper their names from two hundred feet away, and they turn their heads to see what we want. Their ears rotate to pinpoint the direction of sound. Loud, unnatural noises bother them, although they seem to like soothing music. Sounds made by their natural enemies frighten them. Drums played on a speaker system don't affect them, but real drums terrify some of the big cats.

On two separate occasions we hired a dance troupe to entertain park visitors on our anniversary, an African group and a Native American group. On hearing the drums, some of the cats expressed immediate fear. Java stood, head erect, as high as he could stand. His ears faced forward, his nostrils flared and his eyes stretched wide and alert. Fear flowed through his veins. We had never seen this kind of reaction before. What could scare Java? Drums!

In a heartbeat, he jolted backward, gathering his wife and two cubs. He took them to the farthest point in his habitat, where he turned and stared toward the beating drums. He couldn't see anything unusual; a building blocked his view of the performers. But he was terrified, frightened for both himself and his family.

Saginaw, the tiger, responded in a similar way. He trembled alone.

None of the other cats, Saja, Passage or Eclipse, cared about the noise.

I ran to comfort Java, and Prayeri ran to comfort Saginaw. Only our presence partially calmed them down. It took the animals hours to recover.

A big cat's sense of smell is also better developed than ours. Both males and females leave scent markings in and around their territories to warn other predators to stay out. That same scent marking also serves to alert prospective mates when their mating season arrives. Unlike the canine group, sense of smell among big cats is relied on less often to track down potential prey, although they are quite capable of picking up a herd of giraffe or wildebeest if the wind is right.

Sometimes we observe the cats all facing the same direction with their noses pointed in the air. A few minutes later we see a small herd of wild horses coming toward the park.

Big cats also use their olfactory system to analyze smells they find on each other, such as who is in season, or what one has on one's coat, or where one has been and with whom. Individuals who have been away from the group usually get the once over. It's also used by lions to provide safe passage for the cubs born outside the perimeter of the pride. Mom puts the scent of the cubs on the various pride members when she makes her way back and forth from pride to cubs, which are always born a distance away. She takes the scent of the pride members to the cubs, so everyone knows everyone else before they ever meet.

We watched Shanta, Java's first wife, introduce two six-week-old cubs, Jasari and Baraka. They walked right up to him and began to pull and bite his mane. He was very gentle and aware of their fragility.

Their sense of taste is also very acute. We have offered the cats a variety of distilled waters in similar containers, which we administered with eyedroppers. Only electromagnetic charges differentiated the water samples, which had been prepared by a good friend, Dr. Joanne Stephanatos, a practicing veterinarian. The cats have no trouble telling apart the different drops of water. Some they like. Some they don't.

Their sense of touch also sparks instincts. Eclipse, the black leopard, loves to have me pet him. He walks quickly toward me and turns and rubs his back leg against mine so I will stroke him.

He usually turns away from me as he comes, so he is in front of me, facing the same direction. This position is critical to our relationship, since I am a male and in his territory. His wife, Saja, used to frequently come in season. In order for us to be close for any period of time, touch is not enough. We have to avoid looking directly at each other. If our gaze connects and I am in the intimidating position of standing above him, he may attack, forced by the combination of three instincts—personal security, territory defense and protection of a loved one. If he does, he is in the air, leaping toward me with his mouth ready to open and eyes focused on my neck.

During a presentation one day in the spring of 1992, I stepped back too late and his glance caught mine. I was in the middle of a sentence at that moment, and I made the mistake of looking at the audience before stepping back away from the panther. He leaped for my throat. I blocked with both arms, but two canines punctured my right forearm. To avoid vulnerability, I shifted from a defensive movement to an offensive one. I went after him. He moved away and at the same time Prayeri called his name, distracting him. In his mind, the incident was now over. Eclipse had lost advantage, so we continued the program, holes and all.

Normally when Eclipse and I are in close proximity to each other, he avoids looking at me because he desires to maintain our relation-

YOUNG LIONESS SULA LETS HER INSTINCTS MOTIVATE HER NEXT ACTION.

ship. And in a relationship, if only one instinct is evoked it can be countered by intellect, avoiding what could become a dangerous situation.

Intellect is the second area of motivation. That is, rational behavior—the ability to assess the environment, weigh consequences of a decision and make a reasonable choice. The conclusion can countermand the behavior of one primal instinct. In the wild, choices are usually made with survival in mind. Instincts alone can get them killed.

DEAN BLOCKS JAVA'S MOCK CHARGE BY PLACING HIS FOOT IN JAVA'S CHEST.

Big cats have senses acute enough to make proper decisions according to their individual perceptions and desires. They usually exercise a rational process to reach a reasonable decision in a given circumstance. The smaller cats, such as servals, bobcats, lynx and caracals, seem to use a higher percentage of instinct than intellect. They all have instincts used for hunting, and killing is an easy follow-up that brings an immediate reward.

Both lions and tigers require a long two-to-four-year education process to learn how to hunt and kill. Mom uses the instinct of play to teach them. Play is converted as their maturity progresses and opportunity presents itself. Many never learn satisfactorily in the wild, so they starve to death or are killed in the learning process. Learning takes time and practice. Instincts are instantaneous when they are present without practice.

If a four-year-old male lion meets a six-year-old lion with two wives, the youngster is automatically motivated by his instincts to attack the

CHAPTER THREE

larger, more experienced cat. Following instincts alone, the younger lion may lose his life. If intellect intervenes and he quickly assesses the full reality of the situation, he may find a different place to roam.

We've found that while intellect can override one instinct in the big cats, it has little influence when more than one instinct is activated. If the younger cat is married and his wife stands nearby, he may be forced to attack the older lion even though intellect would suggest a slim survival situation. The instinct for mating is compounded by the instinct to protect. The issue of safety becomes clouded and the cat might take an erroneous, deadly direction. Rational thought obtained by learning can be overpowered by combined instincts. We have experienced this situation many times.

In one case, Eclipse, the one-hundred-sixty-pound black leopard, had just matured. He "proposed" to Saja, the spotted leopard, for about two months. Finally she said, "I do," and they did. They enjoyed the honeymoon suite, a beautiful habitat here at Out of Africa. They mated for nine days every two to fifteen minutes, day and night, which is the custom of leopards. Eclipse did not want me in the habitat during this time. He backed me away, and I respected their time alone together.

On the tenth day, the honeymoon satisfactorily completed, Eclipse came to me. The panther glowed, obviously glad to see me, for he rubbed against me many times and nuzzled me more than he had ever done. It was to be our last unintimidating reunion. The following day he sought to kill me. I entered the habitat where Eclipse, Saja, two tigers and a lion resided that day. In the front area protruded a large wooden two-story platform we dubbed the Cat Condominium, which I walked into. As I turned around to go out, I noticed Eclipse defiantly blocking my exit.

His intent had changed from friendly to protective. His eyes looked steely, his head tight against his shoulders and his stance assertive, poised for attack. I felt trapped. With only one way out, the panther focused and crouched as his jet black ears pressed low to his head.

Like a spring, he jumped at my throat, and I blocked him with two hands raised above my head, fists clenched. He careened off my right arm, and I felt two canines scrape by my neck, gouging as they went by but not deep enough to hold. The panther fell to the ground. I stepped away from him, needing space to defend myself and an open area to advance and retreat.

He followed.

I felt shocked that after all our good times together he changed so quickly. I knew I was in serious trouble. Fear flooded my senses. Then came resolve, "I have a right to be here." I determined that the panther would not win or kill me. Then I went after him. This is important though dangerous. If he had perceived vulnerability or weakness in me, he would have instinctually made a second, even stronger attack. The instinct to take advantage would have propelled him to kill me.

Now I had the advantage. The cats taught us a technique using our legs, a side kick. It does no damage but surprises the opponent, which in the case of leopards and other cats is considered a move of respect. I tapped a foot on the side of the panther's neck then backed off. I did this on the other side and moved away. I didn't want to fight him but to show him that just because he has the power doesn't mean he can harm anyone he chooses.

From the other side of the habitat, more than a hundred feet away, Sahara, a lioness twice as heavy as Eclipse, came to assist me. She leaped on the panther. Eclipse couldn't move. He resigned, sandwiched, helpless to even defend himself. The lioness had him pinned flat to the ground! Sahara stalled the conflict with plenty of time for me to get out. I walked to the exit gate, relieved to be safe again.

Afterward, the reason for the attack was obvious—two instincts combined to override learning. The mating had stopped but the protection instinct had not, so it continued to operate when I entered the habitat. In addition, the habitat remained the panther's "legal" territory. Eclipse

GOOD FRIENDS DEAN, ECLIPSE (BLACK LEOPARD), SAHARA (LIONESS),
PRAYERI AND SAGINAW (TIGER).

CHAPTER THREE

defended it. Often the instincts for protection and territory defense go together.

Eclipse had to learn to control his instincts so he and I could continue our relationship. If he could not think rationally, then he would attempt to kill me each time we met. He also had to learn to forgive, because without forgiveness we would have no friendship.

Sometimes I make an error in where to stand with him, and he attacks. Of course, I defend myself and counter with first a defensive move then an offensive one. This technique proves respect and nullifies the contest if broken off quickly. But no one likes to lose. Forgiveness is necessary to return to normal. This I do verbally and with body language, stepping about twenty feet away from him then going about my business as if nothing happened, in the same manner a larger, more powerful animal would.

In each instance, of which there have been many, especially in the colder months as the cats respond to an instinct we call seasonal change, I initiate forgiveness by talking to Eclipse. In audible English, I remind him of our close, good relationship, our fun times together and the importance of controlling his instincts. I say, "Eclipse, I am your friend. Be good. Saja is your wife. Prayeri is mine." As I am speaking, I pull away from him, giving him space so he is not intimidated. The closer I am, the more of a threat he perceives.

After a major combat where we actually become physical, it takes a few days to fully recover our friendship, but it always comes back. If he doesn't forgive me, then I can't be with him anymore. Forgiveness is a choice that allows respect to return, and not all animals choose to begin afresh. Eclipse always has.

Savanna, the cougar, chose not to forgive after she attempted to kill me. Our close relationship broken, she never allowed me in the habitat with her again. Broken bonds are sad, but it takes two or more to have a relationship.

This brings us to the third area of motivation—feelings, the relationships big cats form with those around them. In the wild, this is not often as strong an influence as it becomes in captivity. Most predators are solitary hunters due to the nature of their business. The element of surprise favors lone hunting. All snakes, most lizards, raccoons, badgers, bears, eagles, sharks and most big cats hunt alone.

Groups form only when the advantage of numbers outweighs the importance of surprise. Wolves, wild dogs, hyenas, orcas, sea lions, male cheetahs, young sibling tigers, komodo dragons and, of course, lions all generate predatory advantage by strategic teamwork through strong relationships. Even though the act of eating is not agreeably shared with friends or mature offspring, most members cooperate for a common good when hunting. This perceived advantage serves as a motivation for good feelings toward members of their group. It also promotes bad feelings toward those that belong to competing groups.

In our experience with exotic felines, we repeatedly find that when we caringly supply the cats' personal needs, they respond in a reciprocal fashion. One day Prayeri and I saw Saja, the spotted leopard, running frantically in her habitat. We didn't know what was wrong. From above our heads came a loud blowing sound, like compressed gas escaping. We looked up. To our surprise, we saw a hot-air balloon descending over Saja's habitat. We raced to her rescue.

Saja was panic stricken. The balloon loomed less than a hundred feet above her and was coming closer. The red, yellow and blue aircraft carried a basket full of people, all shouting and pointing. Saja had no escape route.

As we ran to her, I wondered at the probability of such an event right in our back yard.

Saja saw us coming. As I approached, I could see the helpless feeling of terror in the leopard's eyes. She was wild with fear. She ran toward us.

I quickly entered the double-entry area of the enclosure, which prevents accidental escapes, and took down her leash. The lead end I put around my hips, and the chain end I double-latched around Saja's neck.

Saja paced frantically, looking for escape. When I opened the gate, she bolted out as fast as she could drag me behind her. The three of us raced for the house. Saja got there first. I remained a leash-distance behind, and Prayeri completed our parade.

Once inside where Saja couldn't see the balloon, she calmed down. The terror drifted from her yellow-green eyes. Appreciation and gratefulness began to show through. She began to lick Prayeri then me. She couldn't stop. The licks were so abrasive and with such force we winced in pain. We had to rotate our arms, side to side, forearm to upper arm, just so we could tolerate the pain of the leopard's enormous gratitude.

She rubbed us with the sides of her head again and again. Rub and lick—this went on until we finally pulled away from her. It had become a definite case of too much of a good thing. Saja obviously felt great relief and extreme appreciation for both Prayeri and me for saving her from what she interpreted as a fatal encounter. This incident and a few

CHAPTER THREE

others drew her very close to us, close enough to call it love. It's easy to see the feelings that motivate behavior.

One day sometime after that, I worked alone in a habitat with Java. The black-maned Cape lion weighed about four hundred pounds at the time, almost five times the size of Saja. The lion felt playful that day. He looked at me with a fun-loving, predatory stare, and his intention became obvious.

"He's going to jump me," I thought. Big cats delight in jumping everybody.

Java began his charge. I knew he would flatten me if I didn't change locale. His speed increased. I headed for the fencing of his habitat, but I knew I wouldn't make it. He had me.

Of course, the best way to handle a playful lion coming at you is to reach the nearest solid object before the lion does, preferably a fence. Then turn, raise one leg up about head-high and aim it into the lion's chest. Next, block with both arms together so the lion's mouth doesn't engulf your head. It's very effective, but timing is everything. If you raise your leg too soon, you'll have trouble holding it up long enough. If your leg is too low, then you will receive his full impact. If the lion charging you is like Java, his mouth is always open. After a couple of times, you get the hang of it.

This time I didn't make it to the fence, so I turned and blocked Java with both arms as I leaned into him with proper stance, lowering my center of gravity. His size hurtled me backward, and I felt like a bug on a Mac truck. Then he landed on me. My back hit the ground, but I had no pain. I felt squashed under the big lion and far from safe. He could do whatever he wanted with me, and I couldn't stop him.

Fortunately, Saja had taught us to keep our eyes open until just before impact then close them. Frequently there is something we can do to ease our fall. I opened and closed my eyes again before hitting the ground.

As I opened my eyes, I saw Saja leap from a nearby platform and hit the huge lion on the left side. The impact knocked him off me. At the same time, Brendel, the big female Siberian tiger, came running to help. She held Java down. I jumped to my feet and exited the habitat.

The leopard risked her life to save me. She is no match for a lion if he decided to attack her. Saja only weighed eighty-three pounds at the time. She freely chose to save me, even though she knew her life could be lost. I believe this is the definition of the greatest love—to give your life for another.

At other times, Java and many others of various species have inter-vened to save both Prayeri and me. We have observed strong love feel-ings between animals, not just mammals and birds but even reptiles. We have seen great distress at the death of a mate and the lingering demise of the remaining partner. For example, a Chinese water dragon, Indian monitor lizard and Southwest collared lizard all experienced the death of a spouse, leaving the survivor alone. The water dragon and the monitor lizard both quit eating, hid from view and wasted away until death came in about two months. They were not sick, and nothing we did helped. The story of the collared lizards is even sadder.

Here at Out of Africa Wildlife Park, we built an outdoor area for vari-ous lizards, turtles, tortoises, snakes, birds and frogs. It's about seventy feet long and thirty feet wide. It is full of assorted habitats with plush accommodations for even the most selective residents. Among the rep-tiles lived a pair of collared lizards we called Mr. and Mrs. Wyatt. They spent most of their time together.

Because of their beautiful turquoise and yellow bodies and their friendly dispositions, everybody loved them. If you put your hand down to them, they would jump on you without any show of fear. Visitors watched them hop from rock to rock, often sharing the same sunning area. They climbed logs and branches together and were a perfect couple.

Mr. and Mrs. Wyatt were usually out in plain view and lived on the same mound but in separate tunnels, which they closed up at night by backfilling dirt from inside the tunnel at the entrance. Their dirt doors prevented surprise by a nocturnal snake or other predator as they slept. During the day, Mr. Wyatt frequently made his territorial rounds much like a lion does, to hunt and to prevent other male collared lizards from entering his domain.

One day after making his normal territorial check, a monsoon rain-storm deluged us. The next day, Mr. Wyatt did not emerge from his hid-ing place. Mrs. Wyatt walked about as usual, and so did everyone else. Our staff became concerned.

The following day, Mr. Wyatt still did not appear. We looked but to no avail. Several days went by and Mr. Wyatt hadn't shown up. Mrs. Wyatt still came out every day and seemed to show little concern. After ten days, we knew Mr. Wyatt had died. We had turned over everything in the habitat, but failed to uncover him. We finally concluded that he prob-ably died during the tremendous down pour when his tunnel collapsed. We all discussed our collective hypotheses in front of Mrs. Wyatt and expressed our sympathies to her.

LIONESSES SHANTA AND SAHARA SHOW OFF THEIR BEAUTIFUL EARS. ALL BIG CATS HAVE MARKINGS ON THE BACK OF THEIR EARS TO SIMULATE EYES IN THE BACK OF THE HEAD.

The next day she disappeared. Being September, some thought she had gone into hibernation early, which was a reasonable, natural conclusion. However, many of us didn't fully believe that. She knew her husband had died; she left to join him.

In the following spring of 1993, Mrs. Wyatt did not emerge with the other lizards. We wondered if perhaps she had died during the much colder than normal winter. Then one day in early summer, she appeared. We were overjoyed. Our curator of reptiles, Luke Thirkhill, discovered her and brought her out for us to see. But she didn't look the same. Nine months before, she was in perfect condition, but now she bulged, grossly enlarged with what looked like rolls of fat on her neck and a size to match an adult male. Her colors were muted, and she appeared to be in distress. We didn't recognize until later that she had come to say goodbye.

Out of Africa's premiere show, Tiger Splash™, began in August 1993. The play instinct is displayed as tigers, wolves, bears and cougars romp even in water for all to enjoy!

WE AT OUT OF AFRICA SINCERELY MISS THESE BEAUTIFUL SOUTHWESTERN COLLARD LIZARDS, MR. & MRS. WYATT. THEIR PRESENCE BROUGHT MUCH JOY TO ALL.

Luke moved her to another habitat to keep a better eye on her and keep her separate from her twenty-four youngsters that hatched around the time of her disappearance. She went into the ground and did not surface that summer or ever again. We keep pictures of the pair for fond remembrance. Their vibrant, loving way with each other expressed nothing less than a model for us to follow. Even death could not keep the Wyatts apart. As I think of them, tears always mist my eyes.

Animal motivation springs from instinct, intellect and feelings, and the three combine to initiate any given behavior. Adaptive behavior promotes and sustains life. Mistakes in behavior provide food for others, so only the smartest survive. Those who can address an issue and bring it to a satisfactory conclusion live to make another decision. In the wild, events happen suddenly and luck is not always on the animals' side. Well thought-out decisions are vital. As we watch the animals and the decisions they make, we realize that their life skills have application to our own lives. What

ADORABLE YOUNG SERVAL JAMAA SHOWS OFF HIS BEAUTIFUL EARS AND EYES TO VISITORS.

RETURN TO EDEN

is a good decision for them could be considered a good decision for us, for our families and our corporate and social activities. Saja became our first teacher. Through her we learned:

❖ Don't take a greater risk than is necessary when striving toward an objective.

❖ Cover as much of your risk as possible, so if something unforeseen happens you have a retreat.

❖ Never completely expose yourself.

❖ Get close to your target before making your move.

❖ Watch to learn about your target before pursuing it.

❖ Be careful not to choose a goal too big to handle.

❖ Know your limits.

❖ Do not decrease your ability to sense your environment.

❖ Avoid fighting, as loss is likely and gains may be small.

❖ Make friends and secure your position with them so you are not caught alone.

❖ Practice is important.

❖ Develop self-control.

❖ Exercise and practice patience.

❖ Help others and don't expect to be repaid.

❖ Respect the space and presence of others.

❖ Don't force yourself on others.

❖ Show kindness.

❖ Know who you are and develop your potential.

❖ Ask for help.

❖ Go about your business quietly and don't call attention to yourself. That is for others to do.

❖ Wait until the storm passes to make a decision.

❖ Consider tomorrow as well as today.

❖ Enjoy life and do what needs to be done.

❖ Remember your Creator so He remembers you.

LOVE AND NURTURING THRIVE AT OUT OF AFRICA. HERE SIBERIAN TIGER SAGINAW, AFRICAN LEOPARD SAJA AND PRAYERI DEMONSTRATE THAT LOVE TO VISITORS OF THE PARK. FEELINGS ARE AN IMPORTANT PART OF MOTIVATION IN ALL CREATURES, AND THE FEELINGS EXHIBITED BETWEEN THESE THREE ARE A PRIME EXAMPLE OF THAT KEY COMPONENT IN THE PHILOSOPHY OF LIFE AT OUT OF AFRICA WILDLIFE PARK.

In Search of Primal Instincts

O ut of Africa Wildlife Park functions as a learning center. We charge an admission fee but give special rates to educational facilities. We have never sought donations but work cooperatively with local and national businesses. The park and its animals are maintained through revenues from admissions, retail sales, food service, off-site activities and a few assorted profit centers. To this day, we've managed to expand and to pay all of our bills, thanks in part to the management lessons we've learned from the cats themselves.

Because of the warm climate in this part of Arizona, our busiest season extends through the winter months when people are visiting from colder climates. Summer days are too hot for most folks, so we include evening activities, such as the Saturday night presentation that can include dinner, and even a camp-out for the adventurous. Campers spread their sleeping bags around the animal habitats. On those nights, most of the cats don't sleep—they watch the campers. At night, the lions often roar great, organ-quivering bellows that can make the ground itself shake. It's a night to remember.

The primary objective of the park is to learn the way of the wild and those principles that allow life to flourish according to natural plan. We give attention to both physical and spiritual elements. We see both manifested and consider each essential to life. That which is not seen motivates that which is seen. The desire comes before the act.

We seek mutual cooperation between other species and ourselves. We've learned to identify the needs and wishes of individuals who are said to have no voice—those we call animals. A leopard, for example, can only be fully satisfied with its life in captivity if all its physical and psychological needs are met. It must have the opportunity to express itself as it would in the wild.

We begin this quest by determining the animal's natural goals, which are safety, food, space and socialization. The goals that the animal instinctually strives to meet are supported by secondary instincts that automatically trigger behavior that fulfills its purposes.

In the wild, the chase instinct prompts the leopard to stalk and then run after a baboon. The possession instinct automatically causes the leopard to defend her baboon meal from a pack of jackals. In order for the leopard to carry out its natural functions, it must live in a place suitable to its body structure and size, a place in harmony with its subspecies and coloration as well as individual preferences and lifestyle habits.

Leopards like large trees with horizontal limbs for sleeping, food storage, escape and observing the area around them. They like tall grass for concealment when they are moving and rocks and logs to hide behind, making it easier to catch other animals off-guard. They like tall cliffs to hide in and to hide their young in when they give birth and raise cubs. Leopards love to explore, to experience new things, smell different scents, taste a variety of foods and have the appropriate grasses and plants for dietary and medicinal requirements.

Our observations of animals in the wild and in captivity, both personally and through the work of others, have helped to create an appropriate setting for our leopards to live and enjoy their own lives. Our ability to place ourselves in the mind and body of the leopard is essential to fulfilling its individual requirements and to the relationship we have with the big cat.

Regular communication between the leopard and ourselves is vital. Not every day is the same. Needs vary. One afternoon I noticed that

Saja, the leopard, looked as if she had eaten more than normal. She ballooned out of proportion. Sometimes she gets an extra piece of food that one of the other cats doesn't want, but this time she appeared more bloated than normal.

All night it concerned me, and early the next morning I went to check on her to see if the bulge had digested. It had not. In fact, she seemed even larger. Her abdomen had swollen like a beach ball. Her normally clear eyes looked teary and somewhat cloudy. She could still walk but not without discomfort. She needed immediate medical help.

I ran to get an animal carrier, and Prayeri called our primary veterinarian, Dr. Irv Ingram. I placed the carrier next to Saja, and we scooted her inside, closed the door and carried her to the van. As we drove, we could see the obvious expression of pain her swelling caused. Her regular, active, full-of-life behavior had been greatly muted.

When we arrived at the veterinary clinic, they had everything ready for us. We had to act fast. Dr. Ingram prepared an anesthetic, which I injected into her back leg. About ten minutes later, Saja began to lose consciousness, though her eyes remained wide open. We were praying as she went under. We still didn't know what to think. I carried Saja to the operating table, and she drooped limply in my arms. Her head hung down over my forearm as I laid her on the stainless steel table. We turned her on her back and tied her legs to the table with rope to give her better position and balance.

The nurses covered her with surgical sheets but left an opening around the abdomen. They placed two pockets of instruments on an adjoining table and unfolded them for the procedure. Dr. Ingram, now scrubbed and ready, shaved the area he intended to enter. Then he began his incision, one layer of skin at a time.

Carefully, he opened the ballooned abdomen. At first we saw little blood, which was sponged away by one of the nurses. The

ECLIPSE DISPLAYS THE ATTACK LOOK OF THE PREDATOR, WHICH CAUSES THE FIRST PRIMAL INSTINCT, SELF-PRESERVATION, TO AUTOMATICALLY TRIGGER IN HIS TARGET.

doctor increased the incision slice to about seven inches. We could see inside. Her two uterine horns appeared massively swollen. Dr. Ingram became worried.

The infection, though still contained, could easily flood everywhere. He had to drain the excess fluid outside the body cavity. A nurse brought a three-gallon stainless steel pail that we positioned under Saja. Making about a one-inch opening in the most accessible infected area, Dr. Ingram contoured Saja's body, and about a gallon and a half of infected fluid poured out into the bucket.

Then he put his hand inside Saja's body and held up the other uterine horn so the yellow liquid could flow out into the bucket. When we finished, the pail's contents approached the rim—three gallons, about twenty-four pounds of infectious fluid.

Then he removed the two punctured uterine horns and the ovaries. Both he found to be highly infected. If he just stitched her up without removing the diseased organs, she might have been in the same condition again down the road.

When we completed the operation, Saja weighed twenty-seven pounds less. About an hour later, she began to wake up. We had covered her with blankets because recovery time for most mammals is slower if the body temperature drops below one hundred degrees. She roused briefly then went back to sleep. Dr. Ingram and I carried her out to the van, where she could continue her recovery.

She slept the rest of the day and all night. The next morning, she drank chicken soup. After three days, she began eating small pieces of solid food, mostly chicken. Eventually Saja gained back all her weight and is now heavier than she was before.

Since she no longer cycles every couple of months, Eclipse is not as satisfied, but Saja is alive. If we had missed the signs of Saja's distress, even by another hour or two, the horns may have burst, probably killing Saja. In order to fulfill their needs, we have to stay in touch.

Once we know what the animals require, we make it our job to fill their requests. This can only happen when we're willing to see from their point of view. We go to great lengths to be sure all our friends feel comfortable in their surroundings. Every aspect of their lives is given consideration. Wherever possible, discontentment and frustration are avoided.

Most important in these considerations are instincts. Each animal has a prioritized series of natural behaviors that direct their activities toward specific goals. Instincts encompass both defensive and offensive behaviors and are the part of the animal that many people consider unpredictable, the wild side of animals. But with keen observation and close association we've come to understand the predictable nature of animal instincts.

Survival prioritizes instinctual behavior. Instincts are multifaceted and designed to extend the quality of life for the individual and unconsciously perpetuate the species. Instincts work within all life forms and integrate individuals into a whole system where all practice the same process—survival. From cohabiting with animals, Prayeri and I have identified four basic needs that we consider primal instincts.

First Primal Instinct:

SELF-PRESERVATION

Individual security usually rests at the top of the pyramid. A strong enough sense of safety must be attained for an animal to move about freely. A life form that feels threatened often remains motionless. Security overrides even the need to eat. If a tiger captures its prey, it wants to be left alone. Any perceived danger would prompt the cat to wait despite its hunger.

If a lioness catches an antelope and the smell of blood attracts a leopard, the leopard remains wary despite its need to eat because the larger cat could kill the leopard. The lioness' security is not threatened, but the leopard's is because of the lioness' superior position in the predatory structure. However, if the same lioness is confronted by a male lion from another pride, her security becomes threatened. She instinctually gives up her prey to the stronger cat.

At Out of Africa, a comfortable sense of individual security usually runs high in all our animals. The cats are so well acquainted with one another that only occasionally do they steal each other's food. Their personal security is rarely challenged, and the ones who choose not to live together are kept apart. It wasn't until we brought in a male and female king cobra that I fully recognized the priority of this basic instinct.

In the summer of 1994, we acquired an eleven-foot female and a thirteen-foot male king cobra. The two had never seen each other before. Cobras are snake-eaters, even swallowing their own kind after biting and killing the victim. We didn't know what to expect, but we only had one habitat for the two of them.

I let the female out of the bag first, in front of the audience. Then came the male. He was twice her weight. I hedged my bet that they would be all right together because they had been removed from their stable world and taken to an unfamiliar one. We released him into territory currently unclaimed. The probability of him eating her on the spot was greatly reduced, and it gave us time to analyze their relationship. At this point, their first concern had to be individual security, not food.

When the female saw the male, she immediately took defensive action; she raced toward a log, flattened her neck and laid motionless, parallel to it. The log was wider than she was and gave her a larger appearance and a measure of camouflage. This behavior showed her fear and reasoning power. She knew she could be eaten by the larger snake and chose the best protection available under the circumstances.

The male increased his speed, gliding toward her neck, which is normally the primary target. While straddling her, he raised above her almost a foot. Then he dove at her neck. But instead of biting, he stopped and flicked out his tongue just above her head. He analyzed her scent to decide what to do. After about ten seconds, he moved off her, which showed he accepted her presence.

She lifted her head off the log in relief and went about cautiously exploring. Neither snake had eaten for almost two weeks and had missed their normal feeding the day before. A few days later, when they had become familiar with their surroundings and felt individually more secure, we offered them food, which they took.

Second Primal Instinct:

THE ACQUISITION OF FOOD

The acquisition of food, like all instincts, is prompted by survival and is in itself not learned. A tiger doesn't control his drive to acquire food unless there is a reason to stop it. Two such reasons are love and fear. All else being equal, H. G. Saginaw, our six-hundred-pound Siberian tiger, does not eat Prayeri or me because he has learned we are his friends, and he has good feelings toward us, generally speaking. Fear is also a deterrent to the fulfillment of getting a meal. Elephants are large enough to step on lions, so lions—no matter how hungry they are—usually do not consider healthy adult elephants in their prey range. The risk is too great, and the first primal instinct takes precedence.

Often we demonstrate the operation of the second primal instinct in our presentations at the park. Many visitors like to see big cats eat, so we sometimes toss a section of a cow on a high platform in front of an audience. Saginaw jumps onto the platform, anchors the meat with his massive paws and begins ripping and crunching. From his perch he has a good vantage point to see the other cats and us. If one of the

SAGINAW SHOWS DEAN THE DEFENSIVE SIDE OF THE SECOND PRIMAL INSTINCT, THE MAINTENANCE OF FOOD.

smaller cats should wander by, he growls, lowers his ears, widens his eyes and bares his lips to show his teeth—all thirty of them. It's a formidable growl. He has no challengers. It's one thing to read about the ferocity of tigers and another to hear the fearsome vocalizations that come through those menacing teeth.

If the fence collapsed between Saginaw and the audience, the seats would immediately become empty. This kind of intimidation through fear provides valid reason for us to acquire other food besides Saginaw's.

Even though there is a hierarchy among cats, the smaller ones defend their food in the same way, unless there is a relationship between them that is more important than the food dividing them. Saja, a tenacious, hundred-pound leopard, has no trouble keeping at bay the three-hundred-fifty pound Bengal tiger, Passage. When the tiger was a cub, Saja mothered her and Passage still respects the leopard.

In dealing with predators who can choose to eat us, we can learn or be lunch. If a big cat has food, leave him alone; it's his instinct to keep it. Often we demonstrate for the audience what can happen when we enter the big cat's space. I walk toward Saginaw, asking him if he would consider sharing some of his meal.

Usually he turns, eyes glaring. If he breathes backward, inhaling, I know he's ready to leap off the platform to attack me. His attack is not meant to kill but to direct. It is an emphatic command to stay back or he may not be able to control his instinct to protect his food. He isn't playing. It's real, and it's exciting!

I make a hasty retreat and explain it's a table for one.

We use no weapons and have no physical means of defense should Saginaw actually attack me. We have seen him swat both Passage and Eclipse through the air for simply walking too close to his meal. In order to deal with primal instincts that could result in our harm, we've learned from the cats to follow what we call long-term survival principles.

These principles are something like our traffic laws that allow us to drive around instincts without being injured. In the case of the second primal instinct, acquisition of food, the survival principle says, "Whoever gets it, keeps it."

When Saginaw gets the food, he legally owns it. If Passage should happen to get the food first, then Saginaw wouldn't bother her due to their relationship. Instead, he'd go to the one who supplies the food.

The ferocious defense of food can also be modified by the use of another survival principle, one we call the principle of submission. This principle can be observed in other large predators, such as the entire canine group and even primates.

If I walk toward Saginaw as he crunches on his raw rack of ribs and I look at him, stretch out my arm and request a portion of his banquet, I trigger the second instinct. He defends his meat.

But when Prayeri turns her back in a posture of submission, approaches the feeding tiger with head lowered, slowly backing up to him, thinking about things other than his food, he allows her to peacefully stand within a foot of his meal. The survival principle of submission only works if one has a relationship established with the tiger. A stranger would be dessert.

Once food is acquired, the instinct flips to the maintenance side, which in a captive environment expresses itself as warning—"Stay away!" As long as a close relationship exists between the cat and me, I do not consider food acquisition the most dangerous instinct. It can usually be seen and heard and thus avoided. If no close relationship exists between us, then a big cat instinctively defends its dinner.

Third Primal Instinct:

MAINTENANCE OF TERRITORY

Territory is directly related to food acquisition. In order for a leopard to survive, it must have sufficient space to include the prey animals it feeds on. In other words, a leopard will develop and defend an area that has sufficient food most of the year. Some lion prides have small territories only six or seven miles in any direction because there is abundant game and water present. If the same lions lived in the Kalahari Desert, their territory would need to be ten times larger.

Leopards and other big cats scent-mark their territory to alert other predators. What the leopard is saying amounts to, "Stay away. This land is mine. If I find you here, I'll defend it." The material sprayed is a mixture of urine and their own personal scent. It designates residence and is sprayed as often as every twenty feet. When a big cat enters a new habitat, it sprays trees, mounds of dirt and certain already pungent smelling bushes and shrubs as well as walls, dens and large, solid objects. Anything it wishes to claim as its property it sprays. Sometimes that includes us. After a few minutes we can't smell it, but other cats can smell it for days.

SAGINAW MARKS HIS TERRITORY THROUGH THE BEHAVIOR OF THE THIRD PRIMAL INSTINCT, MAINTENANCE OF TERRITORY.

If a leopard or any other big cat has a choice of territorial size, it chooses one as small as possible to support itself. The reason is simple. The greater the territory, the greater the difficulty of maintenance and the greater the risk of chance encounters with competitive neighbors or nomadic predators looking for a home range or following the herds. Nomads, like some hyenas, wild dogs and lions, often travel in groups and have the advantage over the lone territory defender. So it is always best to take only as much as one needs. Greed is not an instinct, nor can it be learned by animals. It's only found in one species—homo sapiens.

Once the leopard claims a territory and suitable living quarters, it will defend it. Occasionally, visitors will ask to come in with us while we are in a habitat with a group of cats. Sometimes they explain how much they love animals and how much animals always love them. Once in a while, someone will even offer to pay us. They feel that because we would be with them, they would be safe. However, none of these reasons would be considered valid by the big cats who consider the habitat their territory.

Cubs are an exception if properly raised. Just about anyone can pet a baby lion or leopard. But maturity brings instincts to the surface as the creature grows.

If a stranger were to enter the natural protective habitat of an adult leopard, jaguar, lion or tiger, the cat's most probable response would be defense of his territory against the intruder. He has no concern for the person's feelings about animals. He's subject to the territorial instinct, and sight alone can activate the defense response. The lion may even perceive the person's lack of understanding as good fortune; the meal has delivered itself.

At Out of Africa, we have guard rails in addition to the tall chain-link fencing around all our habitats. Audiences stay behind the guard rails, an additional six feet away from the habitat fencing. Though the cats can't enter this six-foot zone either, they still consider it theirs.

It's fun to watch one of our own staff people playfully run back and forth in this corridor between the fence and the railing, exhibiting prey behavior. The juvenile cats join in the game and chase with them, but the adult cats take it a little more seriously. For some, this is a possible lunch.

If a staff member kneels down to resemble a four-legged herbivore and turns his back to the cats, sometimes Saja, our spotted leopard, will make a beautiful arch-shaped leap to attack. Since the chain-link screens the person from the cat, it is safe and their presence in the corridor is only a minor infringement on territory. But if someone unknown to Saja enters the corridor, it's perceived as a golden opportunity to eat. Territorial instinct gives way to food acquisition. A defensive instinct transforms into an offensive one. The fear of losing territory gives way to fearless predation to defend it.

In defending territory, killing is not the objective; repelling the intruder is the goal. Even from the intruder's point of view, killing the landlord is less desired than taking over his hunting ground. In the wild, most territorial battles don't end in death unless one of the combatants succumbs to infections from festering wounds weeks later.

Occasionally, visitors to Out of Africa are engulfed in great, bellowing, innard-rattling roars coming from different habitats where our lions reside. Even the buildings shake in the sound blast! Guests often ask why lions roar.

Their roar is connected to the maintenance of their territory. Each bellow is an audible scent-marking, since each voice is as distinctive as a fingerprint. The lion pride is telling all others, especially other predators, to stay away.

CHAPTER FOUR

Roaring is also a location technique. It tells individual pride members where the others are at any particular time. If a lone lioness is away from the pride, she can find them by calling to them. Upon hearing her roar, her pride members will respond unless the first two primal instincts, security and food, are in operation.

Fourth Primal Instinct:

MARRIAGE AND FAMILY RELATIONS, TO BE PART OF SOMETHING GREATER THAN ONESELF, NOT TO BE ALONE

For leopards, jaguars, cheetahs, snow leopards, clouded leopards, cougars and all smaller or lesser cats, males usually have no part in natural cub raising. However, in the case of lions and some tigers, males participate in family activities and are not just motivated by an instinctual sex drive. Both parents take cub-raising seriously.

The father's main role is protection, followed by part-time cub sitter, role model, disciplinarian and finally, king. He is the ultimate authority figure, the indisputable ruler, and his word is law for the pride. Where there is a kind ruler, harmony unites the entire pride. But where there is an insensitive, brutal ruler, psychological and physical injuries abound.

At the park we work hard to teach kindness to all the cats so that when they grow up and a hierarchy develops, the ruler will be a benevolent one. For the safety of all of us, it cannot be otherwise.

When it comes to the instinct of marriage and family relations, the most spectacular and dangerous species is the lion. The behavior of the others is relatively easy to predict and easy to handle, but the lions' social and psychological system is complex and volatile, even to its own members.

In the case of Java's pride, we've seen many variations in marriage and family activities. Java has two wives—Shanta and Sahara. Java was four years old and Shanta was two when they actually married. We saw him "propose" to her on three different occasions.

Java would run to Shanta, head erect, mane fluffed and full, standing tall and being very attentive. He tailored his attitude to assertive without being overbearing. Repeatedly he flanked her, though Shanta always moved away. Java never tired of the pursuit. His sense of smell told him her season had come, and he knew she must be close to accepting him.

Finally, on her third cycle, the lioness said, "Yes." Shanta accepted him as her husband and protector in March of 1989 after we moved to Ar-

TAKING CARE OF THE KIDS, JASARI AND BARAKA, IS
PART OF THE FOURTH PRIMAL INSTINCT FOUND IN
BOTH PRAYERI AND SHANTA.

izona. They mated every five to fifteen minutes for eight days. Java exercised relative gentleness, but he would not allow Shanta to be more than ten feet from him the entire time. He remained incredibly protective of her and charged anyone who came near them, even visitors beyond the guard rail.

Prayeri and I were told to "Stay out!" We couldn't even go in to clean. Both refused food for the first four days. During the latter days, a few pieces of chicken were eaten, but mostly by Shanta. On the ninth day they ate.

To this day, Java's honeymoons are like that. He'll violently charge us with his ears laid back, head down, a blur of speed. Within seconds, he hits the fence near where I stand. It seems the fence won't hold against his speed and weight, but somehow it always does. The fence just doesn't look the same anymore.

One hundred fourteen days after the beginning of their honeymoon, Shanta delivered four cubs. They died of mastitis, which is toxic milk. Dr. Sam McClearan, our veterinarian at the time, ruled out the most common origin of the mastitis, unsanitary conditions. We never did determine how Shanta's milk became septic.

In a couple of months, Shanta came into season again. They went on a honeymoon, and she became pregnant. On November 11, 1989, Jasari and Baraka were born. They were smaller than the previous four but were healthy except for a bacterial infection that proved treatable. In the Kiswahili language, Jasari means bold or courageous, and Baraka means blessing.

We always give the cats names with a specific meaning. It provides a psychological advantage to the creature and to us

YOUNG LIONESS SULA DECIDES TO TAKE MATTERS INTO HER OWN PAWS AS SHE LETS HANDSOME SOLOMON KNOW THAT SHE IS ON TOP OF THINGS IN THIS FAMILY.

as well. They tend to grow into the meaning of their given name. It is like a symbol, a representation of who they are to become, a goal.

Before the youngsters were born, we thought we knew the due date and prepared for their arrival. We had shown Shanta the large birthing den equipped with heater and light, and she wanted to deliver there. Just before Shanta began to give birth, she called for Prayeri to be with her. Sandy Spellacy, who has a wonderful spirit of team work, was stationed outside the habitat Shanta chose for the nursery. Sandy called Prayeri.

When my wife arrived, she sat down next to Shanta. I had been doing a presentation at that moment, so I simply brought the audience to the birthing habitat. The situation grew tense. We remembered the deaths of Shanta's first four cubs, and we knew that the expectant mother could also die. It happens in captivity just as it does in the wild.

Shanta seemed nervous, too. She walked back and forth, first inside the den then outside. Then she'd lie down, then back up for another anxious walk around the habitat.

Prayeri became alert and ready. She wondered if the cubs would even come out. Sometimes only a C-section can save the cubs and the mother, and recovery time for the lioness can interfere with proper bonding to her cubs. Without a strong bond, she could kill her own off-spring or choose to have nothing to do with them.

Even if the birth went smoothly, Shanta might not have any milk or it could again be toxic. After seeing her newborns, she could attack us for being too close, even though we had been together constantly. The instinct to protect youngsters is very strong, and only a stronger, learned reason can keep that instinct from manifesting dangerous behavior.

We waited. Nothing happened. Park visitors waited breathlessly. Everyone pressed close to the habitat guard rail and each other to witness the moment of birth. We even called the media, all the local TV stations and the local papers. One station sent a reporter and cameraman via helicopter. Everyone was ready.

Prayeri and I were inside the habitat when it happened. The pregnant lion went into labor and immediately dilated. She pushed hard each time and then sat down. During each contraction, we could see a dark bulge. Then she stopped and the bulge disappeared. But the contractions came quickly, and in twenty minutes we could see Jasari coming out, bulging further with every push. Finally, in an all-out gush, Shanta pushed the tiny lion, who spewed out onto the den floor. Shanta quickly turned around and ate the sack around him. She severed the cord with her molars and began to lick him all over. His mouth opened and we saw him take his first breath. "He's alive!" we shouted.

The audience breathed a collective sigh of relief. Cameras flashed and film rolled. What a moment! What a relief!

Shanta allowed us both to stay. I picked the cub up to weigh him— two pounds, three ounces. Shanta didn't seem to mind.

Baraka came about an hour and a half later. She weighed one pound, thirteen ounces. Like Jasari, she was flawless.

The cubs' eyes remained closed for a few days, but their nursing instinct began functioning soon after birth. You could see their mouths reflex as we put our fingers up to them.

Shanta let the babies nurse. She was curious and surprised at the miniature lions. She awkwardly picked them up by the head and walked around with them all over the habitat. We talked to her, giving her verbal encouragement and instructions, and in a little while she became more comfortable with her babies. She knew they belonged to her, and she wanted to take care of them. At first, she pushed them around like stuffed toys. When she played a little too rough, they would cry out. She'd stop instantly and reexamine.

That night before dark, I hung a tarp in front of the den and turned on the heater. We brought in sleeping bags, mattresses and pillows for ourselves and blankets for Shanta and the cubs. When I closed the tarp, it held the heat in well. During the first night, Shanta stayed with her offspring and hardly moved. She was exhausted.

On following nights, as she regained her strength, she became more active and even wanted us to "cub-sit" until the wee hours of the morning. She would wait for us to come at night so she could visit Java for a few hours. Always by 2:00 AM, she would call us with a moaning sound so we would let her in. Often she would still have an enormous amount of energy and would expend it on me. Her goal remained the same every night—to put her mouth around my head.

To get her to stop, Prayeri would hold up one of the cubs and tell her, "Shanta, you are a responsible mother. Be careful of your babies." Within a minute or so, the lion-mother would settle down for the night. Most of the time Shanta and the cubs would shift a bit, but not enough for us to wake up. In the morning, I often opened my eyes to find a cub or two on my chest. Shanta would be on Prayeri's sleeping bag, while Prayeri had wrapped herself in a blanket and curled up in a corner.

Usually, we'd all be up by 6:00 AM. Early morning times were the best. The lions were still sleepy and play was gentle. As they woke up, play became rougher and so did Shanta. We'd then gather our bedding and head for the house. For three months we spent every night sleeping with Shanta and her cubs. That wonderful experience passed much too quickly.

When the cubs were about two months old, Shanta wanted to take them to see their father. We watched eagerly as she called them to follow her out of the nursery area to meet with Java in a nearby habitat. The cubs had absolutely no fear. They marched right behind mom and up to their dad.

He had seen them being born and their growing up had been in plain view from his territory at the time. Shanta had rubbed their scent on him and his scent on the youngsters. He knew they belonged to him. He seemed curious and unsure of what to do with these little creatures, who began using him as a big toy. Being very careful where he stepped, he finally walked away. It took about a week for Java to become comfortable with them.

The cubs loved their big dad. They pulled on his mane and chased the tuft on the end of his tail. They jumped on his back as much as possible and even rode him like a horse. Sometimes Java would stand and walk away with one cub still straddling him. Java treated both of them gently. Occasionally, you could see irritation and he would snap at them, but he never touched them with his mouth. From time to time, he put a paw on one and held them down for a brief moment, but never once did he show aggression or ever abuse them.

Most of the time, the cubs played with each other and with their toys under the watchful eyes of their parents. Shanta always knew where they played. During this cub-raising, we noticed that the lioness paid particular attention to human mothers with kids. She watched how they controlled or didn't control them, how far children were allowed to stray from their parents and how parents disciplined their children.

In the wild, uncontrolled offspring are often the targets of predators, so it was natural for her to observe other mothers. She judged human nature compared to lion culture and didn't seem impressed. Humans allow their children to stray much farther than a lion would consider safe for her cubs.

After a year the cubs' play grew rough and unceasing. Even their mother tired of being bitten and jumped.

Java's attention to fatherhood had a more general scope. Designed by nature to be a protector of those he considers his loved ones, his pride and family, he did not need to involve himself unless one of the other big cats nearby caused a commotion. Then he would explode. Java changes position faster than the eye can see and issues directives to his family that are immediately followed.

Once when the tigers, Saginaw and Passage, were tiffing, roaring defensively at each other, it alarmed Java. He ran to his family and told them to go to the furthermost habitat corner, away from the tigers. They responded but not as quickly as he'd ordered. He growled his command again and escorted all three of them. He then turned and came back halfway between his family and the tigers. Widening his stance, he stood glaring at the potential threat, ready to attack any tiger that approached his family. When the tigers stopped their dispute and when he felt satisfied that the threat had passed, he returned to give the "all clear" signal to Shanta and the cubs.

It was obvious to all, Java loved his wife and children. Even food did not often come between them. When we fed the lions, half the time Java would secure the food and stand guard while his family ate. After his family had eaten a sufficient amount, he joined in, never hurting any family member. He often left them the last pieces and watched them at a short distance as they finished their meal.

The cubs grew rapidly and became exceptional in size and appearance. Prayeri and I continued to be welcome in the habitat the entire time Java and Shanta raised them. We played with them constantly, and most of the time they respected us as people. Occasionally Java had to come to our rescue because the cubs joined together in everything they did, including jumping us. Jasari proved a bit unruly, and Java disciplined him as needed, usually with stares, gruffs, rapid swats and mock charges.

Finally, the inevitable happened. The cubs matured to fourteen-and-a-half months old. Jasari weighed about three hundred pounds and was "feeling his oats." He didn't always listen to his dad and had been playing rough with Shanta, too. Because of his size and attitude, we knew that a time of separation loomed close, but Java hadn't yet made a decision on his son's status in the pride.

One night we gave Java the head of a cow, which he had partially eaten, leaving some for the next day. He put it on top of a platform in the show area. In the morning Prayeri and I came in to clean and remove any leftover bones. Java told me to leave his stash alone, so I did. I talked with him and Prayeri about how funny the skull would look during the next show, since it still had all its teeth and would be grinning toward the audience. But I left it where Java wanted it. During the show, I explained the partially eaten cow's head, so as not to offend anyone unused to cow head decor.

Then Jasari came by and saw the food sitting on the platform. He jumped up and began to eat.

Java, who had come to the front of the arena to eat chicken, hand-fed by a staff member, noticed Jasari on top of the platform eating his stash. Java whirled around and charged at his son. Java leaped to the platform, chasing Jasari off. Then Java returned to his chicken.

About fifteen minutes later, Jasari jumped back on the platform to eat the cow's head.

Java spotted him. In seconds he'd mounted the platform.

Jasari fled off the back side and we thought that would be the end of it. Instead, Java pursued the smaller lion and caught him. In full view of everyone, Java grabbed Jasari in the chest and shook him without tearing the hide from the muscle before he let the younger lion go. Java had thrown out his son for disobedience. It happened sooner than normal, but Jasari had grown larger than normal.

We put Jasari in another habitat. He seemed completely bewildered. He didn't understand. Why had his father, who had loved him and always been there to protect him, behaved like this?

His sister, too, was confused and knew the family would never be the same. She had a decision to make. She could stay in her father's pride and never be with her brother again, or she could go with Jasari and never be with her father again. She suffered great distress, and we watched her for the next five hours.

She paced back and forth while still in her parents' habitat. She could see Jasari, who himself was in obvious anguish, alone for the first time in his life. Who would Baraka choose?

Finally she made up her mind. She walked to the gate leading to Jasari and with her eyes asked to be let out. She chose to be with her best friend, her brother. They became almost inseparable and did nothing alone. Baraka visited Java and Shanta a couple of times but stayed only briefly.

Shanta visited her kids, too, but Jasari soon became too wild and played rougher with his mom than she found comfortable. Two months later, they parted company for the last time. The connection had been broken; a new pride had begun.

We gave Baraka a hysterectomy, leaving the ovaries so she would cycle normally but would not have cubs by her brother. This was done prior to her first serious estrus. She would cycle every forty-five to sixty days, which Jasari liked. When Jasari and Baraka began mating, and in lion society became officially married, Java insisted they be removed from his domain entirely. Jasari had become intolerable to him. Male offspring are usually not permitted to mature in their father's presence.

It took about six months to find the

PICTURE PERFECT FRIENDS. PASSAGE, THE BENGAL TIGER, LIES COMFORTABLY BELOW YOUNG SAGINAW, A SIBERIAN.

CHAPTER FOUR

right place. Everyone here loved them and didn't want to see them go. While we searched for a new home for the young couple, Java stopped allowing us to be in with him. Jasari's continued presence annoyed him. Java knew I controlled the young lion's destiny and expected me to remove him right away. He didn't understand that it is more complicated in our society than in his. In Java's world, he'd simply chase Jasari off, not giving a second thought to his son's future; but I was very concerned, and finding the right place takes time. So a wall of separation developed between Java and me. Java put Prayeri on my side of the wall because in his eyes she is my mate and, therefore, one with me. After about three months, Java refused to allow either of us in his habitat. He charged the fence in a defensive behavior.

After much searching, I received a phone call from Rick Schwartz, the director of the Nashville Zoo in Tennessee. We acquired a black leopard cub from him the year before, and he heard we were looking for a home for the young couple. He was having trouble with the zoo's two lions and felt he needed to replace them. He had an older female with claws and a younger male who had been declawed. Usually clawed and declawed cats in a zoo setting aren't compatible. In this case, the female brutalized the male and Rick needed to find separate homes for them. He hoped to keep the female and introduce her to Jasari and Baraka over time, but with the habitat situation he had, I knew it wouldn't work. Lions are cliquish, and the female would have been killed upon entry.

Rick finally found homes for the two he had and refurbished the habitat, which included a waterfall, a pond, lots of grass, giant trees and a big night house. Two animal caretakers from the zoo flew to Phoenix and rented an air-conditioned truck to haul the waiting lions to their new home. A good friend of ours, Rowland Sylvester, built a pair of containers suitable for the trip.

When it was time to go, we opened the doors and both Jasari and Baraka walked inside. We closed the doors gently and eight men barely managed to lift each carrier a few feet to the truck. It was a sad day for us and many of our annual members who had watched them being born, but it was necessary to keep peace with Java.

That's the lion way. In Java's culture, the young males are always removed. They become threats to their own pride. If they are permitted to stay, their father is sentencing himself to death. For they will at some point in their maturity attack their own father to mate with their mother, aunts and sisters. They would also kill any young siblings still dependent on their mother. Even knowing this, it still hurt to see Jasari and Baraka go.

The next day, Java let Prayeri and me into his habitat. He welcomed us, and all appeared forgiven. What a fine reunion. Once more part of Java's pride, Prayeri and I felt complete again.

Six weeks later, Prayeri and I took a few days off and flew to Tennessee to see Rick, Jasari and Baraka. His facilities and personnel impressed us, and the lions recognized us immediately. They looked robust and happy in their new home now, and Jasari had his own kingdom. Already they had gained weight and Jasari's mane had grown. Though leaving saddened us, we knew the lion couple would have a good life, their own kingdom.

Aside from the disharmony between Java and Jasari, another situation unfolded that prompted Java to tell us to stay out of his area. He took another wife, Sahara.

Sahara grew large, weighing about three hundred eighty pounds. She'd been raised by Saja, the spotted leopard, and had lived with the two tigers, Passage and Saginaw, and her best friend, Eclipse, a male black leopard. For a year and a half, Sahara wanted to be with Java but Java refused. She continued to do everything she could to get his attention and affection. While in a separate habitat, she would run about, causing him to look her way. Then she would roll seductively in front of him.

Java would have nothing to do with her.

We thought their union was a good idea, so we began telling Java how nice it would be to have two wives.

We verbally asked Shanta if it would be okay with her, and she seemed to indicate a "yes." She looked over at Sahara, whom she had seen grow up. Her eyes remained calm, peaceful. If she had glared, it would not have been a favorable sign. Both Prayeri and I understood the same message—acceptance.

To find out for sure, we asked Shanta if she would like to spend a

JASARI AND BARAKA ENTER TRAVEL CRATES FOR THEIR LONG DRIVE TO THE NASHVILLE ZOO.

CHAPTER FOUR

few days with Sahara in a habitat together. She immediately got up and walked to the gate near Sahara. We followed, opened the door and brought Shanta into Sahara's habitat where the lioness waited. Neither exhibited hostility toward the other and they stayed together for three days without incident. It turned out to be much better than we expected.

Shanta had given her okay.

But Java still refused. At that time, there seemed to be no point in pursuing Sahara's relationship until Java gave his consent.

Sahara began to pick on her adoptive mother, Saja. Without hurting, she purposely chased and knocked down Saja in Java's full view. She hoped he would recognize her standing as a fitting bride. In the wild, lions and leopards are enemies, so Sahara wanted to show Java her worthiness.

After six months, Java gave his approval. He began to come forward toward Sahara. Before, he would stay away from her, as if not considering her ready for him. He is a king, and in his world only the worthy approach. It became plain to us when Java finally signaled he was ready to receive her.

We put Sahara in a neutral habitat, and then we let in Java. He strutted around for ten minutes or so, went toward Sahara then away. He scent-marked all the trees and bushes, indicating possession, then went to see Sahara.

Even though Sahara wanted the encounter, she was terrified. She seemed rooted to her particular spot. She protected one side by standing next to the habitat fence, and she never sat, as if ready to run in an instant. Each time Java approached, Sahara barked in fear. It sounded like a very large dog barking, but she uttered only one or two barks at a time if Java hesitated. She probably realized he was much bigger close up and could easily kill her.

Killing was not Java's intent. We find that once a big cat establishes its intent or purpose, if not interfered with it does not deviate from that purpose of its own free will. So Java approached in friendship and acceptance.

But Sahara remained afraid for her life. As Java came close to her a second time, she pierced his nose with one canine. She roared as she bit down, but Java silently turned away. I could have put my little finger in the puncture wound. Java licked his nose with his tongue but otherwise seemed unaffected by the injury. He made no retaliation and treated her just the same as before.

After about an hour, things began to settle down. Sahara's barks diminished as she realized that Java was a gentleman. She allowed him closer. He made no overtures of dominance, no bites, no directives or anything that she would consider offensive. The scene became peaceful. They even turned their backs to each other. So we let Shanta in, too.

She immediately wanted to jump Sahara, but we didn't want the ladies fighting. We explained to Shanta that peace and harmony were good ideas, and she should allow Sahara to be with her and Java. They could all be friends, and Shanta would still be Java's number one wife.

This was Shanta's main concern—losing her status. Within a minute, we saw her eyes soften as she listened to our words. She ambled casually over to Sahara. Shanta accepted our advice and stopped attempting to catch Sahara off guard. The two ladies became friends. We allowed the three of them to return to Java's habitat, but we watched in case we needed to intervene. Injuries occur easily and quickly, but no one offended another that day.

Things went fairly well for about a month, but Sahara had ideas about being Java's number one wife. Rivalry still simmered between the ladies. We kept it muted and prevented any injuries.

Then one afternoon at feeding time, Sahara left her piece of food and attacked Shanta, putting one hole through the top of her skull, one near the ear and another under her chin. Java heard the commotion and jumped between them, breaking them apart.

In his domain, he allows no fighting unless he initiates it. Shanta continued to finish her food, and Java sent Sahara away. He gruffed at her as only a male lion can. She knew exactly what he said: "Stop fighting. This is my kingdom. Give Shanta her space."

Sahara immediately hurried away and laid down by herself.

We checked Shanta's injuries and decided to put her in another habitat for a few weeks to recover. However, while Shanta was gone, Sahara made her move. She came in season and flaunted herself shamelessly all around and even on top of Java, pushing herself all over him. She wouldn't take no for an answer. Java resisted her for a couple of days, but it became obvious Sahara was attempting to steal Java's heart and oust Shanta as his favorite.

Java finally gave in and they mated hundreds of times, but not in the same way as with Shanta. He did not stay as close to Sahara, and only a few times did he initiate the mating. The regularity seemed off, as well. Over the days, they'd often go for hours without mating, whereas

CHAPTER FOUR

with Shanta you could set your watch to it. Sahara pushed and manipulated, while Shanta had exuded sweetness.

After three weeks, Shanta recovered and begged to return to the pride. When she came in, Sahara attempted to show dominance and met her with a rough attack but not an attack to kill. Java immediately stepped in between them and backed Sahara down. Java reinstated Shanta to her original hierarchical position.

Never again did Sahara attempt to take over. Shanta and Sahara remained good friends from that day forward. There was little squabbling between them, and they took turns being in season with Java. While one was with him, the other stayed separate. This was how Java liked it.

Beginning in 1992, we saw Java's mating behavior change both with Shanta and with Sahara. We watched him tell Shanta to come into season. He took her away from Sahara, possessed her, causing her to stay with him. He told Prayeri and me to stay out by charging us. If we even came in to clean, he would chase us, just as he had done during the eight-day mating period. But they weren't mating.

It originally took Shanta fourteen days to cycle after she was told. Now it takes less. The whole honeymoon period now lasts two to three weeks. When it is over, we ask Java if it is okay to come in. If the answer is, "Yes," he blinks a long blink. If it's, "No, we aren't quite finished," he keeps his eyes wide open, focused on us.

If we are still in doubt and hesitant, then we seek verification. I step in and Prayeri remains outside, holding the gate. If he charges, we take that as a definite, "No." If his attitude is relaxed and accepting, perhaps

TO BE PART OF SOMETHING GREATER THAN ONESELF—THE ESSENCE OF THE FOURTH PRIMAL INSTINCT IS FOUND EVEN IN KING COBRA ORION.

looking at something else that has caught his attention, then we know it's okay to approach. We don't like to make mistakes interpreting what Java says. It could be costly. The instinct to mate is only partially controllable...sometimes. The right decision is important.

Sahara, too, experienced a change in Java's mating attitude. In their mating in the fall of 1993, Java initiated Sahara's affections. It lasted longer than usual and there was a pause of a few days in the middle. Overall, the honeymoon was much more casual. This is a good sign, as it shows a much more loving approach to their relationship.

Mating actually causes disharmony in the pride. The process itself can be violent. Many loud growls, snarls, and roars can be heard. The third member of the pride feels left out as though she shouldn't be there, which would be the case in the wild.

If Java had another lion for a pride buddy, he would attack his friend first and then begin to mate. That's what he's actually doing when he tells me to leave. It's a warning, and no real damage is intended. We just don't hold up as well as lions do in combat, so Prayeri and I always do as Java commands. When the instinct runs its course, we can return.

The four primal instincts give direction to life and toward a lifestyle that is appropriate to any particular life form, whether it be lion, jaguar, deer, python or fish. All activity can be traced back to one or more of the four. To achieve satisfaction of these four goals requires nine supportive instincts. We've seen how they function in the lives of our friends, and understanding them has enriched our lives.

In Search of
Supportive Instincts

The four primal instincts of personal security, food, territory and marriage and family relations are supported by nine major secondary instincts. These secondary instincts trigger automatically to achieve the primary ones.

Remember, instincts are unlearned, stimulus/response behaviors. They occur if there is no reason to change the behavior. They are like breathing; one doesn't think about taking a breath, it just happens. If you choose to alter the natural response, you can voluntarily stop breathing for a time. Only when you decide to change what is otherwise an automatic behavior will the behavior alter. This is how instincts work, automatically. The secondary instincts kick in to achieve the objectives of the primary ones. They can be suppressed by conscious effort if only one instinct is activated. Combinations of instincts can overwhelm the strongest learned response.

First Supportive Instinct:

SEASONAL CHANGE

Seasonal change is evoked in the wild when there's a sudden drop in temperature. Fall and winter storms can bring it on. The creature will be wilder than normal, and the four previously mentioned instincts of security, food, territory and family relations can all be affected.

A sudden drop in temperature causes big cats to become hungrier than normal because they must eat more to maintain body temperature. Here's how it works: When a major storm blows in, wild animals generally seek shelter. Like us, they don't want to be caught out in

JAVA LOVES PRAYERI, AS YOU CAN SEE IN THE PICTURE TO THE LEFT. HOWEVER, THE WISE KING OF OUT OF AFRICA DISPLAYS THE PROTECTION INSTINCT, WHICH KEEPS THE PHOTOGRAPHER AT A SAFE DISTANCE.

CHAPTER FIVE

freezing rain or blowing wind. If the storm takes more than a couple of days to pass, and the big cats are out of food to maintain normal body temperatures of one hundred to one hundred two degrees Fahrenheit, then they are going to be extremely hungry. The longer they wait, the hungrier they get. When they finally go out, they may be willing to take chances normally considered unacceptable.

The same circumstances occur with their prey as well. Prey animals don't go out foraging and browsing in dangerous weather. Now they, too, are consumed with hunger.

A new alertness shifts the animals' systems into high gear. In order to find food, they're willing to travel beyond their territorial boundaries, entering into unfamiliar country where other competing predators may live. At times like these, when alertness and hunger peak, many animals die.

Storm damage may have changed the prey animals' feeding patterns, making them hard to find. Predators are forced to search in unfamiliar territory for food, and when big predators meet, competition is keen. Raw, uncontrollable instincts are pitted against each other for survival. This is a highly dangerous time of year for animals, especially those living in extreme latitudes and altitudes.

The instinct of seasonal change exists in ecosystems that endure monsoons, such as Asia, Africa and certain desert regions, like northern Mexico and the southwest United States. The monsoons can drop temperatures within minutes, causing many animals to seek shelter. Immediately after the deluge, the landscape teems with wildlife, all looking for food and each other.

In captivity we stimulate a similar seasonal change behavior in a presentation we call "Tiger Splash." We actually swim with tigers and other big cats. The pool is fifty by thirty-three feet and four feet deep. When the cats get wet, they quickly become wilder and less able to control their natural responses. They bite much harder, claw more and hit with greater force than normal. The cats can easily lose control of their ability to inhibit their power and are more dangerous. In this particular situation, the animals must be more conscious of their power, teeth and claws so we are not injured.

Prayeri and I were doing a lion presentation one Sunday afternoon in the fall of 1993. The sky became cloudy and almost overcast. A black, threatening cloud blew in, and a chilly gust of wind swept through the park.

Suddenly, Java's eyes widened, and he whirled around. Wildness surged in the big lion. Prayeri and I started for the gate about two hundred feet away. But Java caught sight of us. He hesitated for a couple of seconds then charged. We weren't going to make it.

I turned and faced him. I saw a big jagged stump between us, so I ran there. When Java arrived, he didn't have a clean jump, so he stopped. Prayeri made it through the gate and was safe. Java and I were alone together.

As quickly as the chilling gust came in, it affected Java. His attention turned toward Prayeri and the gate. As he walked there, I walked next to him, just behind his mane and outside his line of vision. When we reached the gate, I stepped through. Had I been in front of Java within his direct line of vision, he probably would have jumped me.

Our biggest concern was the effect of the weather on Java's fourth primal instinct, marriage and family relations. We had been in with Java's wives, and he might have told one of them to come into season. Between a sudden drop in temperature and Java's need to remove the competition for his lady loves' attention, our career could have ended right there. He would not have been able to control his behavior. The first supportive instinct, seasonal change, added to the fourth primal instinct, marriage and family relations, to produce a near disaster for us. The second supportive instinct, possession, also entered the volatile mix, making the situation even more dangerous.

Second Supportive Instinct:

POSSESSION

Possession is a sliding instinct that manifests with and intensifies others. It is seen when Java protects Shanta, even before she actually comes into season. It is seen in our leopard, Eclipse, when he returns with Saja after their honeymoon and Saja is close to me. It occurs when the cats are eating and they don't want anybody around them. It occurs when even a cub decides to possess a toy, especially if it is soft like a basketball or fluffy like a stuffed teddy bear. The possession instinct can be deceptive, giving the appearance of play, but the result can be an uncontrolled bite or clawing if one approaches too close.

I was in the Tiger Splash show one afternoon with a basketball in the water. I grabbed it and held it as far from my body as possible. Swimming near me, Kipling, a Bengal tiger, watched the basketball and wanted it. He stood up and leaped, raising his left front leg out of the water and striking my right temple about an inch from my eye. One of his claws hooked in and tore open my flesh. Possession of the ball was his primary motivator, but that is the only time I received stitches because of a cat.

Jamaica, a black leopard, loves cloth towels and hangs onto them tenaciously, attacking any other cat who ventures by. Miya, a South American jaguar, even claims possession of a human youngster or dog that she has chosen as her meal, even though the prey is on the other side of the fence and no actual contact is made. Passage, the tiger, sometimes attacks Saja, the leopard, if she ventures too close to Calvin, another Bengal tiger in a habitat twenty feet away. Passage has laid a claim to attack the neighboring tiger and doesn't want Saja's interference.

This instinct is explosive and we keep it in mind as we deal with all the big cats, particularly since we can also be the object of possession. This happens many times and always provides us with a few tense moments. We usually handle this situation with distraction through the use of barter, offering the cat something more desirable than what he already has. A piece of food works well, the bigger the better. If food is unavailable, a larger, more inviting or intimidating object, even another cat, distracts the predator.

MIYA, A YOUNG JAGUAR, WRAPS HER CLINCHED PAWS AROUND HER FAVORITE TOY, LETTING EVERYONE KNOW WHO HAS POSSESSION.

DEAN FINDS A FAMILIAR HEAVY OBJECT WEIGHING HIM DOWN AS JAVA DECIDES TO TAKE A BREAK FROM ROUGHHOUSING WITH HIS PRIDE BUDDY. THERE MUST BE A LESSON IN THIS SOMEWHERE.

Once during a show in Oregon, Java acted rowdy, as usual, and jumped Prayeri, throwing her to the ground. She realized she was in trouble and called for help. I darted in to dislodge Java, but he lifted his lip and snarled at me. Java held Prayeri tight around the waist while she curled on her knees with her head down and her hands protecting her neck.

I had no choice. Prayeri insisted that I get Java off. He weighed about four hundred fifty pounds at the time. Despite his snarl, I managed to put my knee into his side and shove. He reached out and bit my arm. That took his attention away from Prayeri and she scrambled to her feet. The possession ended.

Generally speaking, once contact is broken, the possession ceases. The cat may still have an intense desire, but such desire is much easier to deal with than an instinctual possession.

CHAPTER FIVE

Third Supportive Instinct:

PROTECTION

When one cat appears to threaten the security of another cat's loved one, either a person or an animal, the instinct of protection prompts behavior.

One day, Shanta was playing too rough for Prayeri. Java ran over to Shanta and told her to get off Prayeri and sit in the corner. Shanta immediately obeyed him. The lioness got off Prayeri and walked to a corner of the habitat where she sat.

During a show, Eclipse began playing too rough with me. Saginaw backed the black leopard down. The following week, it appeared to Saginaw that I was playing too rough with Eclipse. The big tiger had been sitting on a platform with Prayeri, sucking her thumb. He jumped from the platform and backed me away from Eclipse.

I saw him coming, teeth bared, ears flat, eyes piercing. It was a good time to move away. Though he did not intend to harm, Saginaw insisted on his opinion: leave Eclipse alone. I felt inclined to agree.

On two different occasions, Sahara, the lioness, sat on Eclipse, the panther, when he attempted to kill me. When a jaguar named Millennium possessed my jacket with me in it, I called for Solomon, a male lion, who came running and took the jaguar off of me.

These incidents demonstrate the supportive instinct of protection in action.

This instinct has one requirement—a substantial relationship with another living being. It makes no difference whether the protector is a social cat, like a lion, or a solitary hunter, like a leopard. Once a relationship is established, the protection instinct becomes part of that bond. We've seen this instinct initiate behavior within as few as four days of two cats meeting each other, regardless of their species or gender.

It's an instinct that can swing both ways, working either for us or against us. If it combines with mating or cub protection, other relationships have a lower priority. The person who might be protected in other situations can be attacked.

Self-preservation, the first primal instinct, and acquisition of food, the second primal instinct, can also take precedence, and the drive to protect can be voided if the cat is eating or feels its life is threatened.

Fourth Supportive Instinct:

PLAY

After cubs have eaten their fill, they are ready for one of two things, sleep or play. Play behavior begins around the third or fourth week. Some individuals merely paw at something, but in the second month cubs begin to get into everything.

At the park, Prayeri and I like to raise the cats in the house with us. This gives them a chance to get to know us, and we get to know them. The more interaction the better. They tend to remain close to those with whom they begin life, but the one who plays with them can become equally important in time.

Ajanii, a female snow leopard, holds the record for living in the house with us—a few days shy of one year. During that unusual time we played constantly. She loved to chase flying stuffed toys. She also loved to catch me if I began to run away from her. She would scamper to grab my leg with her paws, keeping her claws retracted, and she didn't bite hard enough to cause pain. Now that she is an adult, she still enjoys a good romp.

Young big cats absolutely love playtime. If they are not eating or resting, they are playing. They can become bored like any other youngster if there is nothing or no one to play with. The way to the heart of a lion, tiger or leopard is play. In the wild, it builds strong bodies, develops strategies and techniques and creates long-term friendships.

At first play is clumsy, but after a while it becomes fluid and exact. The instinct of play allows litter-mates to hone their skills into expert, calculating strategies with devastating results for their victims. Big cats can become masters at controlled play. In controlled play, no one gets hurt. The cats monitor their size, speed and use of their teeth and claws

THE PLAY INSTINCT IS SEEN AS DEAN INVITES THE ATTENTION OF PASSAGE, ECLIPSE AND SAHARA AS HE HANGS PRECARIOUSLY FROM A SUPPORT POLE IN A MIXED BIG CAT SHOW AT OUT OF AFRICA WILDLIFE PARK.

CHAPTER FIVE

to correspond to a more fragile body and reduced capabilities. If they played with human friends in the same manner they play with each other, we'd have a difficult time considering our relationship fun.

As Ajanii grew up, she monitored the use of her equipment so we could remain close. The more we played, the better she became at controlled play.

Jaguars are playful, but they don't develop running and jumping skills as their main weapons. Because of their extremely stocky body structure, jaguars simply grab their prey and hold on. Snow leopards rely on their incredible leaping ability, cheetahs their speed, clouded leopards their tree-climbing capability and cougars (mountain lions) their pounce.

Here at the park we provide all the cats with toys. The favorite toy of most cubs is the laundry basket. They even like to jump into it and peek through the holes. They probably think we can't see them. Plastic baseball bats, large ropes, basketballs, cloth items and we humans are among the toys cats enjoy.

We avoid raising a cub by itself because they need continual sibling companionship. They themselves become toys for each other. Varying cub sizes and species can produce some surprising results. Jamaica, a young black leopard, has no trouble playing with Taj or Kipling, two Bengal tigers who weigh several times as much as she does. The tigers often catch and sit on her, but they have no intent to hurt their friend, so Jamaica just waits for them to get off.

DEAN, BLACK LEOPARD ECLIPSE AND YOUNG LIONESS SAHARA ENJOY A PLAYFUL ROMP ON A SUNNY DAY.

Sometimes, as one of them charges to catch her, she jumps into the air, banks off an object and bounds away. When they play, they never use full speed, even when being chased by a much larger playmate. They understand each other's intents so there is no threat to life. Play doesn't involve the serious use of teeth or claws.

A mild form of retaliation sometimes happens between them and us. If I pull Calvin's tail, the Bengal tiger turns around and swats at me. The hit is harder than play, and his intent is to teach. He is saying, "Don't do that!"

We find that playing rough and playing gently with both cubs and adults is possible and enjoyable, provided our bodies can take it. Fortunately, both adolescent and adult cats have the ability to control the force they use on us. We watch them hold back their hits and only grab us with their teeth without penetrating. They can be incredibly accurate.

Many times Java has charged me at a significant speed only to slow down just before impact. As he approaches, he raises up on two legs. I race to the fence, turn, put one leg in the air to catch him in the chest and block with my arms to keep Java from putting his mouth around my head. If I miss, it's very uncomfortable inside the lion's jaws... and besides, it's hard to see!

Both Eclipse, the panther, and Passage, a Bengal tiger, have spent a lot of time stalking us then hitting us from behind when we are not looking. Usually the hits are mild and cause no damage, but sometimes it takes a few days to recover.

In certain cases, the play can be extremely rough, much beyond what one would consider acceptable levels of fun. One time, I walked through the middle of a habitat where Brendel, a five-hundred-pound Siberian tiger, lived. She felt playful, and her favorite game was to hit Prayeri and me when we weren't looking—or occasionally when we were.

On this particular afternoon, Brendel crouched very low to the ground, her ears down and her eyes larger than they ought to be. The tension in her body looked tighter than a coiled spring, and I had nowhere to hide. She bounded at me. I waited for the precise moment and lunged to my right. But tigers have a wide "arm" span, and she caught me with her left foreleg. I hurdled through the air backward in a horizontal position. I don't know how far I flew, but I had plenty of time to think, "I hope I land on something soft." It was an amazing experience.

After touchdown, I sprang to my feet only to see her ready and in position to do it again. To her it probably came under the heading of fun. On my page, it came under the heading of terror. In a moment, she

CHAPTER FIVE

charged at me again. She hit me a second time, and I had the reality of an instant replay with no guarantee of the finish. Again, I landed unhurt. I think. She ran away, turned around, lowered herself to the ground and came a third time. But instead of flying lessons, she stood on her hind legs and boxed me. Down I went.

Brendel took off like before, turned around and came back into position. Though my experience here was somewhat repetitive, it was far from boring. My mind was saying, "This isn't happening." My body was saying, "I believe it is."

It amazed me that I wasn't hurt. Just before her fourth charge, I looked on the ground and found my weapon—a twig about eight inches long and an eighth inch in diameter. I had her now! I twirled the stick in my fingers, drawing her attention from me to the movement. I saw her eyes, and her intent changed. Then I stood up and walked out, keeping a close eye on my flight instructor.

Distraction often provides escape. It pulls the cat's concentration away from the target and onto something else. We have used it many times. If the predator is not focused, it will not attack.

You can always tell if the cat is planning attack or play. If you are in one piece with no holes after the incident, it was play. In the case of attack, you'll know.

The relationship is key. If it is solid, and none of the four primal instincts or first two supportive instincts has been triggered, the decision the big cat makes will be influenced mostly by past positive interactions. The look and behavior of the cat will be more casual.

If one or more of the aforementioned instincts have been ignited, danger threatens. Then the question becomes, "How dangerous?"

It depends on which and how many instincts have fired, your vulnerability and, most of all, the relationship. If the animal at that point of decision considers you nonthreatening, you're okay, but if not, you're in trouble. If the animal's Maker doesn't intervene, the best weapon is distraction to change the animal's focus.

It should be noted that ectothermic land animals, those that obtain their body heat externally rather than internally, such as reptiles and amphibians, don't play. The meat-eating species of those groups have an instinct to hunt and kill already built in. They don't need practice to learn food acquisition, so play as an instinct isn't found in them.

Fifth Supportive Instinct:

THE CHASE

This important instinct is to chase that which is running away. A fleeing target triggers an excitement instantly seen in a creature's eyes and quickly transfers to their legs. The focus becomes, "Catch the prey." If they are playing, it usually ends harmlessly. If they are hunting, it can end in death.

We use this instinct in our Tiger Splash program when we run from one of the cats and dive into the water to get away from them. The instinct prompts the big cats to chase after us and even dive into the water in pursuit. Some even pursue us underwater.

If the pursuit is on land and the big cat catches us, they usually grab with their front paws and mouth but do not bite hard enough to break our skin. Normally a prey animal that runs away exudes fear, since fear motivates their flight. However, because of our close relationship with the cats, our running is interpreted as play rather than fear. They run from each other motivated by play, and the chase is taken in that spirit. Distinguishing between friend and prey, that is, between pretend attack and the real business, big cats must consciously hold back their own wild behavior.

MOCK PREY DIVES INTO THE POOL DURING THE TIGER SPLASH™ PRESENTATION WITH ROYAL BENGAL TIGER TAJ IN HOT PURSUIT—THE CHASE INSTINCT.

CHAPTER FIVE

In the bush, the chase instinct is critical to survival. With the eagle, the airborne chase may begin a mile away and proceed at great speed in a downward direction. The shark chases in water, often in an upward direction. The jaguar frequently uses a single jump. The giant African rock python strikes faster than the eye can see. The chameleon begins its chase with a slow, rocking walk and ends with the dart of its tongue.

One day I was in a large enclosure where several giant pythons lived. The smallest one measured over eleven feet and the largest uncoiled to about eighteen feet. One of the reticulated pythons, Lemon, had been sick. She suffered from a neurological disorder that caused her to make judgment errors.

One day, she climbed into some high branches, and when I kneeled under the tree she struck down at my head. She struck with an open mouth, but as she reached me she realized who the target was and closed her mouth just in time to catch my hair but not my head. Lemon realized at the last instant that I was a friend and not food. Since I had not been looking up at the time of the attack, it made little impression on me. I felt it as she grazed my hair and surmised what had happened, but I didn't see it.

The next python chase affected me differently. I was working on a water fixture in the same enclosure. In a corner of the enclosure, Lemon, thirteen feet long and very agile, watched me from the top branches of a tree. I noticed her there, so I turned and said, "Hi." Though snakes have no ears and she probably didn't register my greeting auditorily, I felt better having acknowledged her presence.

I continued working on the fixture.

ORANGE TIGER SAMARA TAKES ADVANTAGE OF WHITE TIGER ELIJAH WHEN ELIJAH'S ATTENTION FOCUSES ON A TOY THROWN INTO THE POOL.

As I knelt there I noticed her coiling about four feet to my right. She positioned herself in a striking stance and looked directly at my face. She had a striking distance of four feet plus, and I was within that range. If I moved to the right or left, up or down, my movement would trigger a strike in the face at about one hundred miles per hour. I remained motionless.

What could I do to avoid the pending attack? How long could I remain stone still? A snake can remain in the same position for hours, but I knew I would have to move before my muscles cramped or began quivering with the strain. I thought if I moved my head and shoulders backward with imperceptible slowness, perhaps she wouldn't detect the motion and I could slip out of her striking range. Six inches would do it.

I began a slight movement backward. Suddenly an open mouth shot toward my eyes. Over a hundred, needle-like teeth penetrated my face from my hairline to my chin and across both cheeks. After the initial thrust, the python pushed forward, opened her mouth even wider and let me out.

I cupped my hands over my bleeding face and called, "Prayeri, could you come here?"

I heard her call back, "Just a minute."

I stood up and walked to the bathroom to see the damage. My hands were full of blood, but all the holes were tiny. I washed and found I had an oval ring around my face, like a picture frame with rounded corners. It was pretty funny.

Lemon let me go when she realized it was me. That's not an easy maneuver for a big python. Their teeth are recurved to the throat and longer than ours. She had to consciously decide that she made a mistake and then take corrective action. Pushing forward released me from her hold. Just like the big cats, Lemon made a conscious effort to modify her behavior in the chase instinct because of our friendship. The chase is common to all predators and essential to their life.

CHAPTER FIVE

Original
PARK MAP
Fountain Hills, Arizona

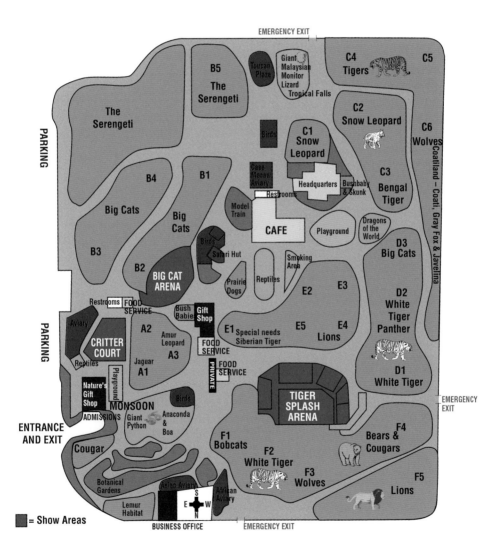

EMERGENCY EXIT

B5 The Serengeti

Toucan Plaza

Giant Malaysian Monitor Lizard

Tropical Falls

C4 Tigers

C5

The Serengeti

Birds

C1 Snow Leopard

C2 Snow Leopard

C6 Wolves

PARKING

B4 Big Cats

B1 Big Cats

Casa Maaaw Aviary

Headquarters

Bushbaby & Skunk

C3 Bengal Tiger

Coatiland – Coati, Gray Fox & Javelina

Model Train

Restrooms

CAFE

Playground

Dragons of the World

D3 Big Cats

B3

B2

Birds

Safari Hut

Smoking Area

E3

D2 White Tiger Panther

BIG CAT ARENA

Prairie Dogs

Reptiles

E2

Restrooms

FOOD SERVICE

Bush Babies

Gift Shop

E1 Special needs Siberian Tiger

E5

E4 Lions

Aviary

A2 Amur Leopard

A3

FOOD SERVICE

D1 White Tiger

PARKING

CRITTER COURT

Reptiles

Jaguar **A1**

PRIVATE

FOOD SERVICE

Nature's Gift Shop

Playground

MONSOON

Birds

ADMISSIONS

Giant Python

Anaconda & Boa

TIGER SPLASH ARENA

F4 Bears & Cougars

ENTRANCE AND EXIT

Cougar

F1 Bobcats

F2 White Tiger

F3 Wolves

F5 Lions

EMERGENCY EXIT

Botanical Gardens

Asian Aviary

African Aviary

Lemur Habitat

S E W N

■ = Show Areas

BUSINESS OFFICE

EMERGENCY EXIT

Sixth Supportive Instinct:

TO TAKE ADVANTAGE

Take advantage when advantage can be taken. This strategic instinct can be observed in predator behavior and is vital to a predator's survival. When the deer lowers his head to drink, when the opposing lion is distracted by other movement, when the play partner turns his back, or when food is left unguarded even for an instant, that's when the move is made. It provides an alert predator with a momentary advantage that is often the needed edge to life or the preview to death. The cats use it frequently on us in the park programs but usually without intent to harm. They often look to catch us off guard.

The best attack is surprise. One waits until the prey is engaged in another activity. If the prey is concentrating on eating, nest building or intently observing another's activity as in mating or courtship, the advantage to the stalker is overwhelming. As a predator, the leopard seeks this advantage in much of its behavior. As a cub, hundreds of hours are devoted to perfecting this insatiable instinct. Of all the big cats, the leopard is best at taking advantage. They are the most successful hunters, because they know when and how to make their move.

Jamaica, the black leopard, easily catches tigers Taj or Kipling off guard. By the time they see her coming she's on them. It's fortunate they are friends. No one takes offense and becomes defensive. Teeth and claws are kept in check.

Seventh Supportive Instinct:

HOLDING AND BITING

Starting several days after birth, big cats bite. They don't learn it. They just do it. Mom and sometimes Dad teach them not to bite. Occasionally, young, rebellious male lions are forcefully removed from the pride by their father if they do not control this instinct. If they are removed early, before they have the necessary skills to hunt and determine danger, then their life expectancy is reduced. They may enter the territory of a rival pride and underestimate the intent, power and strategy of a mature male.

The holding and biting instinct augments the four primal instincts in many ways. On the defensive side of the first primal instinct, self-preservation, biting deters attacking or playing opponents. Biting communicates to a playmate that the fun has become too rough.

In the second primal instinct, acquisition of food, biting suffocates the prey, breaks necks and tears flesh. On the defensive side of the same instinct, as in the case of wolves, snapping jaws and directional bites communicate an unwillingness to share the same table.

In the fourth primal instinct, marriage and family relations, the male uses holding and biting to align the female. The female uses holding and biting to remove the male from above and behind her.

This instinct shows up often when we play with the cats. They catch us with their mouths but maintain control of their power as they learn our pain threshold.

During one evening show, Herb Drinkwater, then the mayor of Scottsdale, Arizona, visited the park with his wife. He brought along a good friend who at the time was editor of the Scottsdale Progress newspaper. I wanted the Lion presentation to go well, but when instincts control be-

havior, surprising things can happen. Every show is different, depending on what the cats themselves decide to do.

Amid the activities that night, Shanta, as usual, felt frisky and came running at me. At the last moment, she opened her mouth.

I blocked with both arms, but she towered over me, looking down with her mouth engulfing the top of my head. I felt overpowered by the three-hundred-pound lioness.

Prayeri stepped in and under the li-

McCabe, a white Bengal tiger, just can't help himself.

oness to push her off. Shanta agreed and got down. At no time did she exert pressure on my skull. She knew her own strength and my weakness. We all knew it was merely play.

We often observe "mouthing" in lions as a greeting, like head rubbing and licking. To be in the mouth of another and not feel threatened shows confidence in a friendship.

Wolves, too, are active "mouthers." They often use teeth to keep each other in check or show dominance in their hierarchy. Wolves use mouthing to give directions, usually when a higher ranking member wants a lower ranking wolf to carefully listen to instructions. It's also used in rescues to pull another away from danger.

Much like human society where hands can be used to express love, to extend help or to brutally inflict pain, animals use their mouths. Holding and biting form an important part of communication and survival. Big cats and other mouthers use the mouth as a point of contact with other living creatures, whether friend, foe or prey.

Eighth Supportive Instinct:

EXPLORATION AND ADVENTURE

Dealing with the exploration and adventure instinct presents the greatest challenge when predators are in captivity. In the wild, this instinct is automatically triggered and never contained. It lasts a lifetime and allows all four primal instincts to function without obstruction. It sends young lions out of the pride when they have learned sufficient skills to fend for themselves. It allows the male and female of any species to find each other in a vast expanse of territory too big for visual contact. It gives the individual animal the urge to find its home range, to establish its own choice of residence, with all the resources it needs to make a reasonable life for itself.

Exploration and adventure provide a variety of prey to meet nutritional demands. They also give a sense of choice that one can control one's own destiny—even if it is a choice to die. Animals have the ability to make choices. In nature, they make all their own choices—where to live, what to do, whom to be with, what to eat, whom to marry and when to go for a walk and where.

In captivity, animals don't go anywhere. They're stuck. When adult animals have limited choice of locale, they often become frustrated and then angry, taking their "island fever" out on other animals and people. Tempers flare, arguments break out. Pent-up anger is explosive. It

HERE IS AN EXAMPLE OF A UNIQUE FRIENDSHIP BETWEEN TAJ, THE WHITE TIGER, AND JAMAICA, THE BLACK LEOPARD. THEY ARE EACH PART OF SOMETHING GREATER THAN THEMSELVES.

causes one to hurt another, to be insensitive and often to be brutal and abusive.

If the need for exploration and adventure is to be met in all its facets, certain conditions must be addressed. The most important factor to an adult animal is self-preservation. It must feel free to be itself without pressure threatening from another. It must also have a variety of foods with enough vitamins, minerals, amino acids and fatty acids to achieve health for a lifetime. It must be free to wander and to choose a suitable domicile with certain characteristics important to itself. And it must be given the opportunity to select its own mate and group of choice. If these natural requirements are sufficiently met, then even animals in captivity can be fully satisfied.

So how do we handle this important natural behavior? It is fairly easy to handle this instinct's aspects in self-preservation, sufficient food and social interaction. But giving the big cat choice in domicile selection is often difficult in small confinements. Aside from an expanded area, as with several national parks connected by free-range corridors, another solution is to connect smaller enclosures with chain-link aisles. If the animal can't see outside its own abode until traveling to another, the scheduled rotation between habitats provides a degree of adventure and exploration.

This concept is now at the intermediate stage at Out of Africa, where enclosures are being joined like links in a chain circling back on itself, so that the park's inhabitants can move from one area to another without doubling back. By opening additional connected areas on a regular basis every day or two, we find this insatiable instinct can be acceptably addressed.

Animals love to go someplace, any place. They also love to come home. If they are allowed to come and go to the degree acceptable to them, then the exploration and adventure instinct can be satisfied to a higher degree.

Ninth Supportive Instinct:

COURTSHIP

The instinct to mate is mandatory to the survival of the species but not to the individual. Some animals live their entire lives looking for a mate when in season but not always finding one. This is more true with endangered species.

Some animals, like bull elephants, radically alter their behavior to satisfy this instinct. They hardly eat and think of only one thing, finding an agreeable partner. Three months out of twelve are spent longingly searching, with scent glands oozing down their faces. They often tread endless miles before they're rewarded. But if an elephant doesn't find an accepting female, he doesn't die. His season passes. He regains the hundreds of pounds he lost and resumes a lifestyle temporarily forgotten. He regains control of his attitude and life.

Other species, like impalas, coatis and pythons, spend less time and energy looking for a mate. However, when mating does occur, much activity can take place, especially if a rival male is involved. In the animal kingdom, sex and violence sometimes come together. First a fight determines the most assertive father. Then the act itself can appear brutal.

One night I witnessed two sixteen-foot male Burmese pythons fighting for the privilege of mating with a fourteen-foot female. Over several nights each python slung the other with the center of his body.

CHAPTER FIVE

THE COURTSHIP INSTINCT BETWEEN TWO KING COBRAS, ORION AND CELESTE—THE DANCE.

SAJA IS IN A DANGEROUS, VULNERABLE POSITION DURING MATING WITH ECLIPSE.

Thuds sounded through the park as each hit the ground. Raising their heads about two feet off the ground, they slapped one another. They pushed against each other, pressing the opponent to the ground and holding him down. Occasionally they would bite each other with their needle-like teeth, but little blood was drawn. Finally, one slithered off and the victor mated with the receptive female. Two months later, she laid about thirty-five eggs.

To animals, the act of mating is pleasurable and also a relief, a physiological and psychological release of the energy that created internal pressure. In the first act of mating, some of the energy is expended but not fully. For lions, mating may occur every five to fifteen minutes, day and night for eight days. Leopards mate every two to fifteen minutes for nine days.

In some species of the big cats and some of the smaller ones, mating is particularly dangerous for the female. Many big cat caretakers know that one can't just put two cats together and expect the female to be alive the next morning. The act of mating puts the female in a vulnerable position. The male is above and behind her, grasping her neck in his jaws. If he is not fully stimulated for mating and considers his territory violated, or has food stashed nearby, he may kill her. A quick twisting bite to the back of the neck can snap the neck without even breaking the skin.

For this reason, the mating act is always short and ends with the female turning around and biting the male or swiping at him with claws extended. This instinctual response protects the female and is the only safe way to mate.

Courtship practices vary widely in animals, but all animals endeavor to achieve satisfaction for themselves, not their partner. Neither do they have motives of perpetuating their own kind. They do it to achieve personal fulfillment, a release of internal pressure. The next generation is a byproduct, not a goal. Offspring result from two, self-oriented individuals meeting their own needs. The greater purpose is thus achieved by the lesser purpose.

In my opinion, this provides evidence of a grand design, one bigger than individuals can manipulate.

ADDITIONAL SUPPORTIVE INSTINCTS

Other instincts assist in the completion of the nine supportive ones. They include the motivation for behaviors such as swimming, domination, socialization and isolation, living on the edge of life and death and tactics such as neck-breaking, backbiting, knee-crippling, team hunting and a variety of species-specific methods of attack and hunting. The behaviors of hunting and killing in themselves are not complete instincts in wild cats. They are learned behaviors triggered by the primal instinct of food acquisition assisted by the supportive instincts of holding and biting, play, chase and taking advantage. Parents teach the activation of these instincts, and their offspring amplify those lessons on their own. For survival, each individual must practice the skills, aided by instincts.

Do They Think?
Intellect and Feelings

Many of us know lions hunt in prides, working together co-operatively to secure prey. In the pride, one female is dom-inant, asserting herself over all the other females and even male cubs younger than about two years old. Only the adult males supersede her.

Usually the lead lioness isn't overly pushy, but rather she is compe-tent and an example to follow. She takes initiative. She is the first to stand at the possibility of food or encroachment. She is the first one to begin investigating and the first to counter an opposing pride. She is the one who takes the lead so that subordinate females—sisters, daugh-ters, aunts—and even mature males, including her husband, can follow and do their jobs properly.

Many hunts are foiled by other members of the pride who mean well but lack awareness and expertise. The dominant female teaches her cubs certain lessons that they need to remember.

First she must teach them to know in various situations which side of the line between life and death they are standing on. They should not willingly cross to the death side except to protect the life of another.

Secondly, she must convey to them that they will have to learn by practicing everything she does. She cannot always hunt for them. Eventually, she'll reach her biological limit to nurturing the grown cubs. At a certain point in their maturity, she will decide to let them hunt for themselves and fight their own battles.

Thirdly, she must impart to them the importance of always keeping watch, for kingdoms are kept or lost in the blink of an eye or the swipe of a paw.

Fourthly, the prudent, dominant female corrects any youngsters if they should break any principles of survival, such as calling attention to themselves while stalking. If any cub deviates, she must be careful to discipline the wayward youth before others see destructive behavior and copy it.

All of this information requires assessment and rational thought, a type of common sense, and all of it must be practiced. Acting on instincts alone is insufficient for long-term survival. The choices made and actions taken based on assessment make a life successful or not. Wisdom is making a reliable choice based on good information that produces an outcome fruitful for the lead lioness and the family. If they emulate her, they too will be successful.

The hunt often requires the cooperation of more than one hunter and an assessment of the prey and the hunting conditions before the chase even begins. Huge Cape buffalo can kill lions, but with accurate judgment and communicative interplay, hunting lions can feast on buffalo. Faulty reasoning means a short life.

INTELLECT:

Do animals think? It's a hard question, and the answer depends on what we mean by "thinking." If the definition of thinking includes the use of higher mathematics or the major alteration of one's environment by abstract, future-based reasoning, then the answer is a definite, "No."

But if it is defined by freely choosing to control the body through understanding the consequences of a decision when those consequences affect one or more parties in the environment, then the answer becomes more positive.

According to Webster, the definition of "thinking" includes the following: 1. To conceive, to form or have in mind, 2. To judge or consider, 3. To believe, surmise or expect, 4. To determine, resolve, work out by reasoning, 5. To arrive at conclusions, 6. To call to mind or to recall.

To be sure we leave no room for ambiguity, let's add the following to the list: 7. Deliberation, 8. Planning, 9. Speculation, 10. Learning—past, present, future, 11. Choice, 12. Acceptance.

If animals show these qualities of a "thinking" individual, then truly, animals think.

To conceive of something is to take it in, imagine and attempt to understand information being received through one or more of six senses—sight, sound, touch, smell, taste or a process I call "discernment" (a knowing or feeling about something without the benefit of outside stimulus, like woman's intuition).

Every veterinary school in the world acknowledges and addresses all five physical senses, which in each species are laid out in the "right places" for the animal to adapt to its environment. If these five sensing devices, which connect to the brain, exist as receptors to retrieve information to support life, then clearly it follows that an interpretive process exists to pass judgments regarding every aspect of survival.

I am going to tell a true story to illustrate the process of thought in animals. I will refer back to it many times in order for us to "see" animals thinking.

At the end of July 1996, Prayeri and I were on a private safari in the Serengeti of east Africa. At about 9:00 AM the second day we came across two spotted hyenas. One was dominant and eating the remains of a Thompson's gazelle. Vultures lunged at the carcass, pulling off strips of tissue despite the protests of the feeding hyena. An eagle also circled the feast, and a pair of jackals darted about, snatching up overlooked morsels.

Through our field glasses, we noticed two approaching lionesses about a half-mile to the west. They walked casually. The pair could see and perhaps smell the meat and the other predators. Though they clearly noticed the activity while they were still further away, the lionesses made no attempt to call attention to themselves or react overtly to what they sensed. However, their gaze and direction fixed on the site of the dead gazelle.

Two spotted hyenas in the Serengeti of East Africa prepare to eat a Thompson's gazelle. They soon find that they are not alone.

Vultures lunge and dart about despite the protests of the feeding hyenas.

An eagle flying overhead (above left) eyes the prey the hyena does not want to relinquish.

Two hungry lionesses, having spotted the vultures circling, close in on the prey.

CHAPTER SIX

The dominant lioness picks up the pace and races toward the hyena, which grabs its prey and takes off. But the hyena knows it is a lost cause and drops the gazelle before the lioness can catch up to her.

The hyenas watch helplessly.

The lioness takes her prize away from the other scavengers in the area so she can enjoy her meal in solitude.

The submissive lioness walks away as she surmises she won't be able to share the prey with her more powerful companion.

As the two obviously hungry, lactating lionesses reached about a quarter-mile from the festivities, one of them picked up her speed, out-distancing the other, who continued walking at the original pace. As the first lioness drew closer, she again increased her speed. About three hundred feet away, she accelerated to a slow run of about twenty-five miles per hour.

The feeding hyena continued to eat the carcass until the lioness approached about a hundred feet away and closing. The hyena held tightly to her food as she whirled around, carrying what remained of the mostly eaten gazelle.

The lioness gave chase.

Before the burdened hyena had run a hundred feet, she dropped her prize lest the lioness catch her.

The lioness scooped up the fallen prey in her mouth, allowing the hyena to escape. Pausing for a moment, she sprinted away from her companion lioness, who had joined the pursuit and still loped about two hundred feet behind.

The second lioness stopped, observed the situation, then sat down, looking in the direction of her companion, who continued running away with the fragmented gazelle. The second lioness ignored the hyenas.

Meanwhile, the dominant hyena and her companion, who had also run for safety, both turned around and loped halfheartedly toward the first lioness.

The jackals had scattered, as did the vultures and the lone eagle.

Finally, the two hyenas broke off the follow-up and returned to the original dining location, followed by the other scavengers. After a quick search for food, the hyenas walked off together, leaving the jackals and vultures picking about for scraps.

The first lioness took the gazelle about a quarter-mile east, away from all the other animals, and ate undisturbed.

Animal thoughts can be seen in their actions.

1) *To conceive, to form or have in mind: All the animals involved obviously had in mind two objectives: obtain food and protect it. The animals conceived future, present and past as thoughts and made decisions based on their individual perceptions and expectations. When the first lioness arrived, the dominant hyena ran for her life but realized the lioness wanted her food rather than to kill her. Dropping the food would save her.*

2) *To judge or consider:* The retreating hyena had to consider her options in dealing with the more powerful, fast-approaching competitor. The hyena dropped her gazelle remnant when she decided protecting it from the lioness was impossible. In doing so, she demonstrated cognitive anticipation of various outcomes. A hyena with no thoughts, considerations or judgments would have continued to feed herself despite the approaching lioness.

The first lioness changed her speed three times; the second lioness didn't assist or pursue; the submissive hyena didn't eat; the eagle left first. All those behaviors demonstrate personal judgments made by each animal.

3) *To believe, surmise or expect:* The first lioness acted on the belief that she could take the prey from the weaker animal, and the dominant hyena expected to lose her catch if the lioness got too close. She expected the lioness to stop chasing her when she dropped the gazelle. The second lioness and the submissive hyena both believed the more powerful animals would prevent them from eating. And they were right.

4) *To determine, resolve, work out by reasoning:* Before the lioness began her assault, she walked leisurely with no goal other than breakfast. Then she saw an opportunity to satisfy herself. The first lioness determined the easiest and most straightforward way to solve her hunger problem and followed through.

Stopping in the middle would have yielded no acceptable results. Reasoning guided her at each stage of the chase until she sat comfortably eating by herself.

5) *To arrive at conclusions:* The animals in our story considered two major areas of importance—the value of the food and the value of their own lives. In drawing conclusions, they weighed the food and their lives against how close each was to a dominant predator.

The jackals, vultures, and eagle correctly concluded that they would not be able to take all the prey for themselves, but they could obtain a portion of it if they persisted in offensive and defensive courses alternately.

6) *To call to mind or recall:* The submissive hyena and the second lioness made no serious attempt to satisfy their own hunger. The reason, of course, is learned fear. They were not born fearing their respective companions. They learned it through experience, experience they recalled at the time of this incident.

7) *Deliberation, carefully considering alternatives before making up one's mind:* How deliberate did the first lioness have to be to insure success? What if there were five hyenas instead of two? What if the food had been too large to carry away? What if the gazelle had been alive and kicking? What if other hungry lions had seen the prey? What if her cubs followed along with her? Cubs have their own free will and often accompany mom on hunts. What if her companion was a male? Would she have been able to keep the food even if she obtained it first? In order for any animal to survive, it must fully understand the consequences of its actions, no matter how many variables are present. Animals must deliberate to survive.

8) *Planning, a detailed formulation or vision before executing a project:* The first lioness did not race toward the food when she first discovered it. Instead, she proceeded at the same pace, although with slightly more alertness than she'd had before she became aware of possible good fortune. She intentionally held back her athletic ability until such time as seemed more profitable. She divided her assault into five stages—walking, two speeds of acceleration, retrieval and retreat—all with minimal effort for the attack plan.

9) *Speculation, hoping to take advantage of an expected but risky venture in order to make a gain:* All hoped to take advantage of the dead animal in order to benefit either themselves or their loved ones. Speculation is the essence of this story.

10) *Learning (past, present, future), to acquire knowledge or skill by study, experience or instruction:* This story demonstrates implied learning. It is well documented that merely being born a lion does not enable an animal to hunt. It acquires knowledge and skills in three ways: watching others (usually their mom and aunts), experiencing "safe" predator-prey situations personally and personal instruction from adults. These learning experiences have a beginning but don't end until the animal itself dies. There is always a new technique or problem to solve. In order for an animal to survive it must be able to remember what it has learned and apply that skill "on the hunt." It its current knowledge proves insufficient for success, it must discover new methods for success. Its future depends on it.

11) *Choice, the privilege of selecting through the power of free judgement:* All the animals in this story came together through individual choices made. Each proceeded in its own way according to its own perception of risk management. None was forced to satisfy or withhold anything. Each made choices.

12) *Acceptance, to acknowledge the reality of:* Acceptance in this sense indicates self-consciousness or an awareness of one's po-

sition in comparison to others. This awareness encompasses the degree to which one can change the players or the outcome to benefit self or loved ones.

When the first lioness took the food, the dominant hyena knew she probably would not see it again. She trailed after the retreating lioness, but her efforts were futile. She accepted her powerlessness to change the situation, stopped her pursuit and resigned herself to her loss. She accepted her condition and her status as a lower-ranking predator and moved on with her friend and her life.

All the other animals did the same. They acknowledged and accepted their present condition and moved on, hoping to discover another opportunity in the future.

From our story, which is commonplace in the animal kingdom, it is apparent that animals do think according to our own definition of the word. This, however, does not mean that they all learn at the same rate. They do not. Some life forms, like predatory reptiles, don't even have to learn to hunt and kill. They already know it through instinct. Bobcats require less training than lions when learning how to make a living. Their prey is usually less offensive, so their personal risk is lower. Hoof stock, such as antelope and warthogs, learn faster during the weeks after birth and then slow down in their learning as they mature.

Generally speaking, the smaller the animal the more often it can rely on instinct and less on intellect. If a behavior can be handled safely by instinct, it is; but intellect must be present to make the crucial risk-minimizing decisions to survive.

Yes, animals think. They have and use an intellectual capacity to modify their own behavior and the behavior of others around them.

FEELINGS (Emotions):

Webster defines feelings as "any of the subjective reactions, pleasant or unpleasant, that one may have to a situation," and the word "usually connotes an absence of reasoning." Emotion "implies an intense feeling with physical as well as mental manifestations." Feelings might also be considered personal likes and dislikes, both physical and psychological.

From the dictionary definition and the actions I've observed in our animal friends over the years, there are four areas in which animal feelings can be confirmed: pleasant, unpleasant, physical and mental.

ECLIPSE BEGINS HIS CIRCLE TOWARDS DEAN IN THE RIGHT PHOTO, WATCHING HIM CAREFULLY AS HE APPROACHES (BELOW).

ABOUT THREE FEET AWAY ECLIPSE VEERS AWAY FROM DEAN TO AVOID EYE CONTACT.

DEAN PETS ECLIPSE AND LEANS TO THE OPPOSITE SIDE SO ECLIPSE DOESN'T SEE HIM EXCEPT WITH HIS PERIPHERAL VISION.

DEAN THEN
BACKS
AWAY TO
LESSEN ANY
PERCEIVED
THREAT.

SOMETIMES A
DISTRACTION
IS NECESSARY.

If you could see Prayeri and me enter the gate into one of the animal habitats used for programs, you'd see Saginaw, a large male Siberian tiger and Eclipse, a male black panther (leopard), come to greet us. As we step in, Saginaw pushes his head against Prayeri then against me.

Eclipse also maneuvers himself into position to be petted. He's affectionate, rubbing himself against not only us but also Saginaw. As we walk toward the front of the habitat where the audience is waiting, Eclipse walks too close to Saginaw and the panther snarls.

Saginaw moans.

Eclipse looks at me and rumbles, saying, "Keep your distance."

From outside the habitat fence, a staff member calls Eclipse by name, distracting him so I can pass.

Prayeri sits on a platform in front of the crowd, and Saginaw follows, pushing himself against her head. He then grabs her thumb with his mouth, sits down beside her and begins sucking on it with a rough tongue.

Eclipse walks towards me, watching me carefully as he approaches. About three feet from me he turns away, faces the audience and lies down with his feet under him. He doesn't look at me. I kneel down directly behind him, stroking his head, neck and back. After a couple of minutes he rumbles, indicating his authority over me. Within half a minute, he's turning his head backward to see me.

I gently but firmly hold his head and lean to the opposite side so he doesn't see me except with peripheral vision. Within another ten seconds, I move back about ten feet and to the side.

Eclipse stands now and rumbles as he approaches me.

I back toward Prayeri and Saginaw.

Eclipse veers away toward the audience. When Eclipse stops at a safe distance, I return to a more center stage location. But Eclipse turns and, seeing me alone, comes quickly. His eyes are focused and hard, and his pace quickens.

Prayeri calls, "Eclipse!" So do one or two of the staff members on the outside of the arena.

The panther is distracted and turns toward one of the staff members who may have something he wants more than me. One of them has a hard rubber toy attached to a rope. They slip it through an opening in the fence and Eclipse clamps down and moves to the center of the arena to hold and protect his possession.

Meanwhile, Saginaw still sucks Prayeri's thumb, which is becoming a little raw. Beneath her hand, resting on her thigh is a towel for soaking up tiger drool. She leans closer to Saginaw so her microphone picks up the slurping, sucking sounds of a contented tiger. Prayeri continues to tell the audience a bit about Saginaw and some other interesting tiger facts and feats.

By this time, Prayeri's thumb is in pain. She asks me for the tiger's favorite toy—a blue, thirty-gallon plastic drum.

I roll it toward him, but there's no response. So I pick it up, placing it just to his right.

Saginaw releases Prayeri's thumb and growls at me then bites clean through the drum. After playing and sitting on it for a few moments, he releases the drum and steps toward the corner of the arena in hopes of getting something to eat, even though he knows he won't be fed at that time.

By now Eclipse has tired of holding his toy and is ready to trade it for a piece of meat. If the piece is big enough, he trades. If not, he waits for a larger one. We make a trade and he crunches down the meat and bones. It takes only seconds. After finishing, he wants his toy back. To get it, he's willing to jump and chase after it, even leaping high off the ground and doing back flips. He'll do whatever it takes to get his toy. Occasionally that means landing on the unsuspecting Saginaw, who protests with a deafening, directional roar. The sound terrifies Eclipse and he leaps backward. Though Eclipse doesn't like Saginaw's reaction, he is powerless and submits to a higher authority.

What I describe often happens as part of one of our big cat shows, and it illustrates animal feelings—likes, dislikes, physical and psychological. All the actions of these cats result from their conscious choices and their instinctual responses. They act in any manner their instincts, thoughts and feelings direct.

Both the tiger and the panther greeted us when Prayeri and I entered. The cats displayed open affection based on their favorable association with the two-leggeds in their habitat. Mentally, they chose to like us. As they rubbed against us and each other, we reached down to pet them, and they in turn pushed against our hands and legs, returning the physical, favorable contact.

As we walked toward the audience, Eclipse got too close to Saginaw and snarled. He disliked the closeness and expressed his disapproval.

CHAPTER SIX

SCOTT BURNS
CHANGES ECLIPSE'S
FOCUS FROM
DEAN TO A HARD
RUBBER TOY—HOW
FORTUNATE!

Out of all the vocalizations available to him, Saginaw responded with a moan, as if saying, "Oh, don't let it bother you."

Whenever Saginaw sees Prayeri sit down, he immediately proceeds for her thumb, which he has nursed on since he was a baby many years ago. He does this because he likes it. Sucking on her thumb provides him comfort, a sense of oneness, a feeling of belonging and a continual reminder of his love for Prayeri. He sucks for as much as an hour at a time.

When Eclipse came to lie in front of me, he came because petting feels good to him. He likes it. Psychologically it helps keep our risky relationship on the "okay" side. But when he becomes satisfied with being petted, he grows restless and looks around. He got what he wanted, and now he perceives me as a threat in his territory. He now dislikes

This toy is mine.

Debbie Kennedy offers Eclipse a piece of meat, which he trades for his toy. This is a conscious choice by Eclipse to get what he wanted more than what he already had.

CHAPTER SIX

H. G. "HAPPY GUY" SAGINAW GREETS PRAYERI AND DEAN AS THEY ENTER THE HABITAT TO DO A PRESENTATION.

PRAYERI SITS ON THE PLATFORM DURING THE MIXED BIG CAT SHOW AND SAGINAW FOLLOWS, PUSHING HIMSELF INTO HER HEAD. HE THEN GRABS HER THUMB WITH HIS MOUTH, SITS DOWN BESIDE HER AND BEGINS SUCKING ON IT. HE HAS ENJOYED HIS NURTURING SINCE HE WAS A BABY MANY YEARS AGO.

SAGI RELEASES PRAYERI'S THUMB AS DEAN DISTRACTS HIM WITH HIS FAVORITE TOY, A THIRTY-GALLON PLASTIC DRUM.

my presence as a male and rumbles. He is stating his superior position and is losing his reason for allowing me to stay.

As I move away, I lessen the threat. I go to Saginaw knowing he'll protect me. Eclipse has no authority over the dominant tiger. When the panther is distracted and changes his attention and direction, I return to my original stance. Eclipse takes offense, displaying a defensive fear prompted by annoyance.

At this point his focus must be broken and distraction works well. The panther's dislike for me turns out to be less than his "like" for a hard rubber toy. How fortunate!

When Prayeri finished her chat with the audience, I brought Saginaw's drum. He wanted it more than Prayeri's thumb, and he growled at me, irritated that I was playing with his toy. If I had reached out at that moment to pet Saginaw, he would have snapped at me with gleaming teeth. He would also have controlled the pressure so as to teach me a lesson without injuring me. His degree of unfavorable feeling toward me is proportional to his bites. Serious anger rarely flares up in our people-animal relationships. But when it explodes, there's no mistaking it.

When Eclipse traded his toy for a piece of meat, he made a conscious choice to acquire what he wanted more than what he already had. The food provided more physical and psychological satisfaction to him than the toy. When the food was eaten, he again desired the toy and was willing to extend effort to obtain it, including a confrontation with the dominant Saginaw.

Saginaw's deafening roar again terrified Eclipse, and he leaped away. Saginaw was angry. Though Eclipse didn't like it, he knew he was powerless to change it.

Such demonstrations of feelings and emotion weave throughout the animals' daily activities. Their feelings come through the intellect and through instinct. They are both favorable and unfavorable, offensive and defensive. If one traces their origins, they spring from the four primal instincts: self-preservation, food acquisition, territory defense, and marriage and family relations.

The degree of response balances between love and fear. If you anger a tiger by stepping on his tail, he may control his negative emotion and hold back his power out of respect for you.

Feelings provide motivation for doing something or not doing something. If the tiger tempers his power, it's due to his good feelings for the transgressor. But if the tiger dislikes the offender to begin with, then the opportunity to terminate the relationship might be considered.

Feelings are important behavior motivators along with logical thought and spontaneous instinct. Feelings join us together. They are the glue between all living, thinking beings. Inconsideration shows the absence of respect for the feelings of another and should be avoided in a relationship. Good feelings make good relationships.

Principles of Survival: The Traffic Laws of Nature

Animal behavior is not random. There are reasons for every action or reaction. Animal behavior follows a design that leads to a continued healthy life. When behavior fails to achieve this goal, blame can be traced to overactive instincts, confusion and inescapable circumstances.

Wild animals live in a dangerous world. Few ever mature or reproduce, because others compete with them or eat them. The two primary causes of animal death, apart from human intervention, involve starvation and being eaten by others. All animals are destined for the same end. The question is not, "Are they going to die?" but, "When?"

This is where the principles of survival fit into the design. Essentially they are learned dos and don'ts, a set of principles that enhance survival. They are integral to both the offensive and defensive sides of the four primal instincts and are like traffic laws that allow animals to maneuver around the instincts of others. However, the individual must choose to use them, and usage is made easier by practice and habit. Predators who master the majority of these natural procedures eat those who don't. Prey who master these traffic laws live longer than those who don't.

The following represents a substantial portion of this design for longer living. The next ninety-nine procedures work together to give life, and give it more abundantly. These principles are like gravity; they have effect whether we believe them or not. Not only do they work in the animal world between individuals and groups; they also work in human society, from families to business. These principles for longer life automatically trigger responses in others.

PRIMARY PRINCIPLES

1. *Obey the authority above you.*

   The leader of a herd of Cape buffalo earned his position in a competition of survival techniques against his own kind, a type of Olympics, by knowing where to find water and grass, when danger lurked and where to run. He makes few mistakes and, therefore, others obey him.

   In a broader sense, animals are completely obedient to their Creator. They live in perfect accord with the plan and purposes encoded within their species and for them as individuals.

2. *Love your neighbor as yourself.*

   When a lioness is being attacked by a pack of hyenas, her good deeds toward her companions will bring her help. But her inconsideration of others will leave her to defend herself, alone.

3. *Be obedient to your parents and teachers so you will live long. They did not successfully mature by not knowing how.*

   The Thompson's gazelle mother makes her newborn infant stay under her so he won't be noticed. The youngster is obedient and his chances to survive against predators are high.

4. Do not steal. (This principle is often broken in the animal kingdom. It can lead to bad feelings, injury, starvation and death.)

One lion steals the food of another but is injured in the attack. The lion becomes infected and three weeks later dies. Stealing was more dangerous than catching his own meal.

5. Do not covet your neighbor's mate, territory, possessions, dwelling or food.

When a contending male lion enters the territory of a successful pride leader to take what doesn't belong to him, he risks his life. It is safer to seek what is not owned and be satisfied with it.

6. Do not murder. (Kill only what is necessary.)

The cheetah chases after one in a herd of gazelles. Because the cheetah kills only what it needs to survive, the remaining gazelles can live to reproduce for the next season's hunts.

Animals don't premeditate the destruction of their fellows. Attacks happen, driven by instincts, but killing is not planned through intellect.

7. Do not destroy the environment in which you live.

This principle is violated when man restricts animal movement. Without human interference, animals move on or die before they exhaust the resources around them. Enough is always left so the environment can be replenished.

8. Conserve your resources.

When the rattlesnake strikes, he only injects enough venom to do the job.

A hunting lion uses the minimum amount of energy, carefully gauging the strength and distance of the prey.

9. If you are not the authority, be his friend.

The second male in a wolf pack is safer if he does not challenge the alpha male but is instead protected by him.

10. Follow your instincts but judge with intelligence, discernment and the wisdom of your emotions.

Leopards don't attack lions in defense of territory and possessions. They can live longer by paying attention to what they know about lions.

CALVIN, (LEFT) A YOUNG BENGAL TIGER, GETS A FIRSTHAND LOOK AT SAGINAW, AN ADULT SIBERIAN TIGER.

CHISUM, A THREE-MONTH-OLD MOUNTAIN LION, ENJOYS THE PLAYGROUND.

CHAPTER SEVEN

PRAYERI AND
PASSAGE POSE
FOR PICTURES FOR
THE FIRST PARK
BROCHURE.

RETURN TO EDEN

11. *Do not reduce your awareness of your environment.*

The cougar does not stalk prey when it is sick. A snake does not hunt when it is shedding.

An animal does not intentionally reduce his ability to sense his environment, unlike humans, who consume drugs and alcohol knowing the debilitating consequences. When an animal's perceptions are dulled because of circumstances, it waits before going into dangerous situations.

12. *Forgiveness is a requirement in a relationship.*

As a pride of lions eat a kill, they often inflict injuries on one another; but when the meal is over, they lick and clean each other's wounds and all is forgiven.

These twelve primary principles provide respect through love and fear. Without respect, an animal is vulnerable. The primary principles establish love. Disregarding these principles results in fear. Love is gain. Fear is loss. Love binds a relationship, while fear sparks distance in a relationship.

All twelve principles have the power to evoke one or more of the four primal instincts, either offensively or defensively depending on the decision made by the animal. The following eighty-seven principles of life can be considered supportive. They, too, engender respect and enhance one's life. Many more principles exist. Paying attention to these brings the others to light.

S U P P O R T I V E   P R I N C I P L E S

1. *Know who you are—your species, capabilities, vulnerabilities, instincts and relationships.*

All animals know their own and know who they themselves are. Their instincts make it plain. Tigers have tiger instincts. Jaguars have jaguar instincts. They act according to the preset plans that are unique to their species.

They must know their capabilities, their speed in comparison to others, their awareness level, whether they are terrestrial, aquatic or arboreal. Lion cubs who get trounced by their litter-mates are less likely as adults to attack others. They've discovered the limitations of their fighting skills.

Animals must also know what they are not good at, their vulnerabilities and where they are weak. If their eyes are in the front of their head, they cannot see behind. If their eyes are to the side, they cannot focus for distance and direction as accurately as if their eyes were in front.

They must know their friends and their enemies. Lions have many friends. Leopards have few.

2. Know why you are alive—your purpose in life.

Every animal that ever existed accepted its purpose for living. Each animal has its place and remains in its own niche.

3. Know what you are doing and why, as well as where it may take you.

An animal must know the type of creature it hunts and what that creature can do. It must study enough to know how the creature will react under various circumstances. If it attacks when it should wait, the outcome could be death.

4. Seek wisdom and understanding so your fears will not keep you from reaching your potential.

A wildebeest calf following its mother on migration must learn to swim the river or be left behind. It learns to overcome its fear of the water and to see itself safely beside its mother, or it is washed away by its fears.

5. Know which fears are instinctual and which are acquired. (It is our fear that holds us back.)

The lion on the plains of the Serengeti watches a man walk toward him with a strange stick. He sees a brilliantly colored umbrella opened up quickly in front of him, and it startles him. The Masai standing there is not a threat to the lion. The lion has seen Masai before, but the umbrella looks dangerous. He has no instinctual memory to understand the umbrella.

If the lion learns the umbrella is harmless through repeated encounters, he may learn that his fear is unnecessary. The umbrella is believed harmless and, thus, he may attack the man.

6. Look for the reason one is doing something, not just what he is doing. (Then you will know how to respond.)

In a swamp, a raccoon hides in a tree while watching an alligator dig a hole on the bank. The raccoon remembers the spot and re-

turns again the next night. The hole has been filled in, and the alligator has gone. If the raccoon investigates the reason for the hole, he'll find a tasty clutch of newly laid eggs, but he better think about where the alligator went and why. If the alligator comes back before the thief finishes raiding her brood, the raccoon might be the meal instead.

7. *Emulate those who are successful in the hunt for life. (It is easier to follow than it is to lead.)*

   When youngsters imitate their parents in the animal kingdom, they learn by example. The parent squirrel teaches the youngster how to forage for its food. So does the bear. If the youngster watches and is motivated by hunger, then it will quickly learn strategies for satisfying its need.

8. *If you are a leader, you must do what seems right even when others disagree. (If you are right, they will follow.)*

WHEN MATURITY IS REACHED JUST AFTER MARRIAGE (USUALLY BETWEEN TWO AND THREE-AND-A-HALF YEARS), A SENSE OF KNOWING REALITY OCCURS. ECLIPSE NOW SEES THAT WHAT HE THINKS AND DOES HAS CONSEQUENCES.

Lions are chasing a herd of wildebeest. To the right is a hill where two more lions sit. To the left is a ravine and beyond that another group of wildebeest. The leader of the herd must make a decision to turn left toward the other group or run straight ahead past the sitting lions. Prior experience and discernment of information are required in being a leader.

Although the herd may want to jump the ravine, the leader may remember that in the past lions have laid in wait in just such places. His experience may prompt him to avoid the ravine and run past the sitting lions. If he's been successful in the past, the rest will follow.

9. Do what you say. (Hope broken is not easily regained.)

A herd of elephants needs a lot of water. If an older female establishes herself as leader, it is up to her to find the moisture and food the herd needs to survive. She must live up to her promise to lead them in life-giving places for their continued following.

10. When you are with others, remember that their opinion counts too. (Respect their opinion, space and property.)

Zebras stick together. They are more solid and secure as a herd than wandering as individuals. When they have disagreements among themselves—about who will mate with whom, who will

LIVING WITH OTHERS, EVEN OTHER SPECIES, REQUIRES RESPECT FOR THE FULL EXPRESSION OF OUR POTENTIAL TOGETHER.

run lead—they give each other respect for their rank within their society.

11. The "I am better than you" attitude causes loneliness and eventual isolation.

Sometimes in herds of animals such as packs of wolves or prides of lions, there is a member whose attitude initiates quarrels. He causes disagreement rather than cooperation. He wants his own way without respect for anyone else, and he destroys relationships rather than building friendships. He prowls the edges of the family group and comes in only to bother and to harm or even kill.

Eventually, after absorbing his arrogant abuse, the members of the group retaliate, returning to him the same irritation he fomented. They chase him out, and he can no longer participate in the nuzzling and grooming. No one will assist him in his time of need.

12. Remember "The Cycle of the Struggle": peace, awareness, desperation, forgiveness then peace again. (It is the fabric from which life is made. While you are alive the cycle will never end. You will see it again and again. If you do not complete the cycle, you are locked into each incomplete circumstance. Forgiveness is the most important part. Holding a grudge will affect all your activities, and revenge is the pathway to death.)

On the plains of Africa, the peace, awareness, desperation, forgiveness then peace cycle is played out constantly, sometimes daily. This cycle promotes life for those who can survive. It also takes life for those who cannot get away.

13. Remember the past, for it will come again.

Animals are creatures of habit. They come where they're rewarded. If they've had a good experience, they return to it. If bad, then they tend not to come back again.

They must remember the animal that they couldn't beat, for if not, they may contend with him again.

14. Earlier learning interprets new information. (Be sure what you have already learned is accurate. Otherwise new, more accurate information may be misinterpreted or rejected.)

When an animal learns how to get food and water, it tends to repeat the same performance. If there is a drought, it may have to dig deeper, but this additional effort requires discernment and learning. If there is no water at all, then the old information of simply digging in the dirt will not satisfy the thirst. A new place will

CHAPTER SEVEN

have to be sought. If the habit of simply digging is greater than the ability to change one's mind, then the animal will reject additional learning and may die.

15. Remember, wisdom is not found in an abundance of information but in the use of that information.

The more experiences animals have the greater the grab bag of possible outcomes. Choice is necessary.

A leopard during the rainy season only has to walk a short distance before it finds food. Prey animals increase when water and grass are plentiful. In the dry season, prey animals decrease. The leopard has to walk much further and take chances with other territory holders. It must choose how best to make its living according to its past experiences and its assessment of the present.

16. Listening (yielding to new, accurate information) is essential to survival. Hearing alone is of little value.

If the gazelle hears the rustle of approaching hyenas, that information matters little unless the gazelle acts on it and bounds away.

17. Discipline and practice enhance ability, and one's equals help develop one's best. A vision inspires both.

A litter of cubs plays, topples each other and practices making a living, having fun, chasing, taking advantage where advantage can be taken—all the activities for growth and maturing. When they see their mother hunt and catch food, the cubs are inspired and can put those practiced abilities to profitable use.

18. Success comes through constant struggles and determination. (Failure is always available, but triumph belongs to the strong and is achieved one day at a time. Choose the easier targets first.)

The young constantly search and play, developing their skills, never ceasing, continuing to practice. They never give up for long. They always return and become strong one day at a time. Their mother brings them small prey. They play with it and they practice hunting before they eat it. As they grow, their mother brings them larger prey until finally they catch their own. Then they are on their own, independent. They schedule success.

19. Sacrifice is a part of success. (Achievement requires a price usually equal to the level obtained.)

While hunting, a lion can be injured; kicks, bites and bruises all occur in the act of hunting. The animal makes sacrifices so it can *eat. The greater the hunter the more experiences he's had. Leaders have more scars than newcomers.*

20. Take advantage of what comes to you each day, for tomorrow may be filled with other concerns.

    If it is dry and there's no water, antelopes don't wait for more rain. They drink whatever they find as soon as it's safe. Tomorrow may bring a pride of lions who will block access to shrunken water holes.

21. Do not worry, for worry is a paralysis of the mind that leads to failure. (Instead, form a plan and carry it out one step at a time.)

    Worry in animals can be seen in pacing when they're afraid and on the defensive to get out. It builds stress. Even a rhinoceros in transit can die of stress. If the animal relaxes and enjoys the ride, there comes a point where the ride is over and the rhinoceros can walk out. This can happen when discernment overrides instinct and the individual chooses to expect a good outcome.

22. Collect the necessary information before making the decision.

    The deer bolts and takes off running. That move alerts the hunter who sees the deer and shoots him. If the deer had remained quiet and low, he could have watched the hunter move and remained safe.

23. Listen to others; they may have good advice.

    The mother, the father, the older siblings, the aunts, the uncles are all good teachers. They have gone farther on the journey and are more likely to be correct than the youngster.

    A lioness who is an apt hunter has successful techniques that a willing pride-mate can emulate.

24. Listening is often better than talking, for talking helps another but listening helps you.

    Animals listen before they make their move. They need to know the probable outcome, for their life may depend on it. By remaining stationary, they're less likely to be seen. If they simply broadcast their position, they're likely to die.

25. Patience is. It is not restricted by time. Don't be hasty or you may miss the path. Remember, animals don't live in time; they live in eternity—and many are successful.

Animals have to wait for that which they need. It does not just come to them. They must put themselves in the right place then wait for the moment of advantage so that they, too, can survive.

26. *Look for the lesson in every occurrence.*

If a lioness becomes trapped by a pack of hyenas and is attacked but narrowly escapes, she'll remember not to be encircled by hyenas again.

Sometimes the worst circumstances provide the best lessons.

27. *Put your effort where the most profitable outcome is found, but don't neglect the rest. Work the weakest area until it becomes strong.*

Grazing in a well-watered area may provide food aplenty but also an abundance of predators. Dryer areas may have poor grass and fewer competitors, but dry gives less nourishment. Animals must be on guard and weigh the risks for the most profitable outcome.

28. *Stay within your "prey range." (Don't take on more than you can handle.)*

A python out for a hunt sees an impala. The python must judge the weight and accessibility of the impala to place it on the prey scale. If it's the same weight as the python, it's within range. If the impala is greater than the python in size and weight, then he can't swallow it and could be injured in the process.

29. *Do not take more than you need or you will become a slave to it.*

LEARNING HOW TO DEAL WITH EACH OTHER BEGINS AT AN EARLY AGE. HERE BABY LION SOLOMON WONDERS WHAT PRISTINE, THE AMUR LEOPARD, IS DOING TO HIM.

Should a lion attack an elephant and somehow manage to kill it, he could not eat it all. Other animals would smell the carcass and come in to take their share. Then the lion would have to defend his kill. Undue stress and possible loss of life could be the result for the lion.

30. Announcing one's position or plan is not always wise. Where there is competition or opposition, silence is best.

   Lions don't roar when they hunt. Predation is silent. They don't tell the prey that they're coming. They don't tell the hyenas that they're present. They just come and kill quietly.

31. Do not contend with little things. Keep focused on your objectives.

   A stalking lioness deals with flies. They land. They itch, but the lioness doesn't scratch. She can't take her eyes off the wildebeest. Otherwise she will miss her best chance for a meal.

32. Laziness causes one to feel worthless, which leads to poverty and a life wasted.

   There are no lazy animals. Animals live and move according to their need. Laziness is not part of their society.

33. If you want something another holds dear, the price will be high.

   A hyena stealing prey from a lion can pay with his life. The hungrier the lion, the more danger for the hyena.

34. Do what needs to be done. Do not procrastinate.

   When a lioness sees nearby grazing impalas start to run, she doesn't wait. She immediately acts. She is already in position to meet her objective.

35. Timing is important. Advantage is necessary in survival.

   The stalking mountain lion must be close enough to charge and pounce. Too slow or too late before the prey takes off and the mountain lion may go hungry.

36. Caution is sometimes the rule. (If the cost is too great, don't do it. Always have a way out. Expose as little as possible. Conceal vulnerability. Avoid conflict whenever possible. Be sure the value of the action is greater than the risk to be taken.)

   From a leopard's point of view, it is better to be treed without food and water by a pride of lions than to risk going down on the

chance of outrunning them. Avoid the conflict. Let the lions leave first.

37. *To be safe is a decision then a reality.*

    The leopard in the tree can decide to stay and be safe, but first she must weigh her chances. Decision comes before safety.

38. *Compromise is better than injury or death.*

    In a pride of lions, differences can arise over who eats first and who mates with whom. Opposing a stronger animal can cause injury or death. Better to be a friend than an enemy.

39. *When you are clearly the lesser, submit to the greater authority and become his friend. Be important to him and he may lift you up.*

    Animals that live in groups, such as lions, wolves and iguanas, have a hierarchy within their social structure; one is above the other. If you are the friend of the one who is greater and follow his directives, you will live longer. If you do not pose a threat, he may even invite you to his feast.

40. *Analyze experiences; they guide decisions not yet made.*

    This is the essence of learning. Animals remember the sights, sounds, smells and outcomes of their experiences. If the outcome was rewarding, they will repeat the experience. If the outcome brought pain and disappointment, they may reconsider and choose a different course of action the next time their senses register a similar situation.

41. *Distinguish between friendly and unfriendly.*

    When unrelated tigers come together in the wild, they make sounds called poofing, or chuffing. These are friendly sounds, announcing congenial intent. If the other tiger does not poof back, it is not friendly and should be avoided. Harm may be intended, not friendship.

42. *Narrow down information to determine a course of action. What is seen and heard is not necessarily what is.*

    As animals approach a new habitat, an area they have not been in before, they approach cautiously. They need to determine the measure of safety and risk. Just because all is quiet doesn't mean there's not a predator hiding in the bushes that cannot be seen or heard.

43. *Decisions must go forward to prosper. Do not look back.*

Once a herd of zebra decides to run, they're gone. Anyone who slows down might get caught. No one pauses to look back. They keep going until they reach safe territory.

44. Don't make the same mistake twice.

    Taking on a larger animal in the same way, having lost the first battle, makes life harder than it needs to be.

45. Do not allow effort to be confused with objective.

    The giant anteater doesn't dig holes in the dirt just for the sake of digging holes. It directs its efforts toward a particular objective: ants. It doesn't waste energy on useless activities.

46. Focus first. Then make your move.

    In all predation, focus comes before the attack. There is no attack unless there is first focus. The objective must be clearly in mind.

47. Familiarity and nonthreatening experiences decrease learned and instinctual fears.

    When a bear learns that it can swim, it must overcome its own fear of drowning. It practices what it has learned, and the successful experiences decrease the instinctual fear of drowning in deep water.

48. One will never learn if one doesn't pay attention.

    Animals are always listening. Their ears rotate. Their eyes notice the smallest movements. They sense the environment. Smells prick curiosity and memory. They pay attention to avoid death.

49. Remember to prioritize your activities. All activity is not equal.

    Self-preservation is more important to an animal than the territory it is standing on.

50. Know the primary instinct you evoke in another and also yourself.

    If one tiger ignores the scent markings on the boundary and breeches another tiger's territory, it can expect a fight. The defending tiger may fight to the death, but if the intruder runs away, the defender will only chase as far as its boundary.

51. Be meek, maintaining your power within control, for it brings many to your side.

Saginaw, the Siberian tiger at the park, maintains his control by his presence. He does not need to kill the others around him, though he has the power to do so. Instead they appreciate his control and become his friends.

52. The flexibility of our hearts opens our minds.

When one animal is introduced to another, fear sometimes beats in their hearts. To remove the fear the animals must gradually sense each other and communicate nonaggressive intents. When fear subsides, friendship can develop.

53. Limits are self-imposed decisions.

When Pristine, the leopard, lost her leg, she learned to walk, run and leap with only three limbs. She continued to play with the other big cats and is a source of inspiration to many physically challenged people who come to the park.

54. Keep only what can be handled with your fullest attention.

Lions have many offspring. Keeping track of all of them is difficult. Only the ones that can be attended to survive.

55. Carelessness can cause loss.

After a kill, lounging around with it invites other predators to come. If the lion wants to keep it without fighting over his possession, he must put it where it won't be found.

56. When we are not gaining, we are losing.

If a squirrel does not gather enough food during summer when food is available, it will starve in the winter. Its loss does not come all at once but in the squirrel's hour of need.

57. Take everything that is known and use it as experience, because everything has a teaching of its own.

The young leopard learns from every competitive engagement and each attempt at gaining prey. It must remember every change and nuance in the situation in order to survive.

58. Balance is essential for life. Mind and body must have a common tune. Budget and balance activity—work, rest, play, exercise, study.

An animal does not run for the sake of running; it runs for the sake of catching food, for preserving itself or for play, which hones skills and enhances relationships. It must also eat and rest so it can do these things again.

59. *Effort must be fruitful and efficient.*

    If a chipmunk is looking for food, it will search the area that produces the highest return. Too little reward drives the chipmunk elsewhere. The animal knows intuitively that too much effort beyond the value of the food can bring on starvation.

60. *We are a product of our choices.*

    Choosing to dig a shallow burrow could mean early death. A warthog needs to judge the depth of its home so predators cannot get to her or her children.

61. *Go about your business quietly. Exposure can mean unnecessary risks, loss or failure.*

    As a leopard walks through a forest, he never announces his presence. There may be a lion in the bush waiting for him. Why should he expose himself to death?

62. *Discipline extends a life, but love gives reason for living.*

    If an animal has the habit of protecting itself and is alert to the danger of the day, it extends its life. But a long life has little meaning without the love and joy that family can provide. Having youngsters to care for gives reason for the extension of its life.

63. *Submission lives longer than arrogance.*

    The leopard respects the hyena. The leopard bows to the lion. The lion yields to the bull elephant.

64. *Love, peace, joy and hope are decisions made regardless of circumstances.*

    An animal takes each day as it comes, one moment at a time. It does not know what the next moment will bring, but it rests in the confidence of life in harmony with the Creator.

65. *Do not take all you can. Leave some for others and tomorrow.*

    Animals take what they need, what is sufficient for them to live that day. They may store enough to get them through the winter, but they only take what they will use. To hoard more is wasted effort.

66. Know the condition of the environment around you. (Risk is unstable and often changes with little or no warning. When danger is seen, take refuge.)

The element of risk has a tangible quality in the animal kingdom. Animals can sense when their lives are in danger. They protect themselves by acting cautiously. Usually, hiding is safer than being in the open, but distance and stillness are their own hiding places.

67. Know when to resign from an endeavor. (Losing more may prosper another. When the probability of your loss is greater than the probability of your gain, you have gone too far. Stop.)

When two animals are fighting over food, they could continue, but one is usually stronger than the other. It is best to resolve a conflict by moving away if you are the lesser creature. If you do not, it could cost you your life.

68. Enjoy what you have. (More may not be better, just more complicated. Live today.)

Even in a time of drought, many animals simply take what they can and enjoy the rest of their time. They still play. They still groom one another. They still chase and carry on all their customary activities.

69. Take time to play often.

Play is an instinct. Some mammals play all their lives. Their life is worthwhile because of their play.

70. Discernment is the sixth sense.

Animals are experts at detecting what can't be seen, heard or sensed in any other way. This discernment gives information about the environment that goes beyond the five senses.

The impala might discern, feel or sense a lion's presence and come to alert attention even before its ears or eyes register the danger.

71. Associate with those who seek wisdom and understanding and are kind.

The leaders of the herd become wise because of the good decisions they make. They have understanding, and the best ones treat others well and teach them the ways of discernment.

72. Do not associate with those unable to control their ways, or your end may be volatile and premature.

Some lion prides are more dangerous to live in than others. Some are more violent. Some have learned ways that cause their early death by violating the lives and territories of others.

73. Do not make the path of another more difficult.

    When animals teach their children, they teach their children in order for them to be independent of the parents. In this way offspring are offered an easier life.

74. Do not condemn another. (He, too, is just passing through and is full of troubles, like you.)

    Animals do not condemn others; they just pass through. They handle situations as they come. At Out of Africa we seek oneness with both animals and staff.

75. Do not reduce awareness of one you care about.

    Animals do not decrease their awareness but increase it. Mature lions out hunting rarely do anything to distract the other hunters. Cubs learn to be part of the hunt, not a detriment to it.

76. Do not favor one over another under your care, for each is competing for your approval and will seek to reduce another in your eyes.

    All offspring compete for the mother's love and attention. If favoritism is shown, one becomes strong but the other weak.

77. Do not fight the battles of one who needs to handle his own situation.

    As animals come up the ranks in a herd, it is necessary that each one expends his own effort to attain the position. It makes him a better survivor and more able to maintain that position against all up-and-comers.

78. Just because your group breaks the Principles of Survival doesn't mean you should.

    Sometimes the herd runs off the cliff. The majority of the herd is lost. Only those following their own discernment rather than that of another are saved in such situations.

79. Be careful who you allow to join you, for the deviance of one will deviate others.

CHAPTER SEVEN

Animals have the ability to learn. If they allow others with a non-survival orientation to come in and join them, the group may choose ways that are destructive to their own safety.

80. Do not do for your children what they should do for themselves.

   Every successful animal parent must teach its offspring to survive on their own. If the lioness continually provides food for her cubs even after they are large enough to do their own hunting, they may die without her, and her efforts to bring them into maturity will be wasted.

81. Let your children go when it is time.

   The mother cheetah is with her offspring for about sixteen months. Then one day she just walks away. They're playing, and when they stop she's gone. They must survive on their own. If she has been a good mother, they have the skills to survive.

82. Do what is admirable so others will see and do likewise. (Remember, you are an example for others.)

   The parents of young animals demonstrate survival skills and principles. The youngsters watch, practice and do the same. If those skills are admirable, the youngsters have a greater chance for a longer life.

83. Helping your neighbor brings you closer to him.

   In a troupe of baboons, if one is injured, the other ones assist him, cleaning and licking his injuries, bringing him comfort when he needs it. Thus he is able to return the favor at a later time.

84. Know which side of the line of life and death you are on. (Do not willingly cross to the death side except to protect the life of another.)

   Protecting the lives of others occurs frequently among animals, for their offspring, their mates and their friends. They sometimes have to die so their loved ones can live.

85. Always keep watch, for kingdoms and lives are lost in the blink of an eye.

   Predators often hunt at night. Prey animals must choose wisely the times and places they sleep. The animal that sleeps when it should be awake is soon found with terror on his face.

86. Don't mistake differences for lack of intellect or sensitivity.

Several differences between man and animals are advanced consciousness and creativity, written language, mathematics, reliance on time, religion and idol worship, pride, greed, lust, lying, morality, intentionally reducing awareness through detrimental substances, premeditated murder and suicide.

Animals have none of these. These concepts do not exist in their minds,

87. *Don't ignore the principles of survival; they are pathways in the hunt for life.*

Those animals who do not learn the principles of survival are the food for those who do.

These two lists of primary and supportive survival principles are by no means all-inclusive. There are countless more. Principles are common denominators of experiences we all have. They generalize a lesson, derived from many similar situations, and are useful in determining the most probable outcome of a decision. Principles are guides to making choices. They can benefit us as well as the animals.

In the End

DEAN AND
CALEB, AN ADULT
COUGAR, SPENDING
A LITTLE ONE-
ON-ONE TIME
TOGETHER.

O n the evening of September 18, 1995, Prayeri and I leash-walked Caleb, a nine-year-old male mountain lion to a new habitat constructed to bring out the instincts of the wild-by-nature animals living at Out of Africa Wildlife Park.

Because the park personnel were still putting the finishing touches in the mountainous habitat and Prayeri and I would not be at the park in the morning when the staff arrived, I needed to place yellow occupancy chains on the gates to alert everyone that this habitat contained a cougar. The habitat has three double entries, a total of six gates, which had to be secured so no one could enter.

We walked in with Caleb on leash. Prayeri closed the first two gates, and we proceeded with Caleb still on leash. We casually ambled to the second double entry and I secured it. We walked to the third. After stepping outside, Prayeri filled a water bowl. Suddenly, she had to go to the restroom.

I said, "Go ahead. I'll unleash Caleb, double check the first entry gates and come out."

Prayeri left.

I unleashed the cougar and began to walk toward the first gates. Immediately, a feeling of great risk came over me, a present sense of danger. This feeling is common in our experience, since our lives are often on the line. We attempt to gauge the level of risk so we know what or what not to do.

I couldn't see Caleb. He vanished into the twilight. But in situations where we release a cat in a new habitat, the response is always the same. The instinct to explore and find adventure takes control, and an excited state of fun and frolic takes over for the next hour or so.

I still had Caleb's leash in my hand, and I thought, "If I run into a confrontation, I'll twirl the leash. Hopefully, that'll distract Caleb." Besides, I had done combat with Caleb on two other occasions and had defended myself in what he considered a respectable manner. Because he could not dominate me, he stopped. Each of the previous encounters ended peacefully.

The circumstances were different this time. It was dark. I wore sandals and had a leash in both hands. The terrain was mountainous, full of many locations to ambush, and Caleb had the advantage.

After analyzing the situation, I felt a compulsion to proceed anyway. I cautiously stepped down the path and hugged the fence line. At the big mesquite tree, I rounded the northern section of the habitat and could see the gate, my exit. Within twenty feet of the gate, practically home, I noticed Caleb crouching low in a ravine about a dozen feet to my left. I froze, unsure of his intent.

He had never bitten me or anyone before, although he loved to ride on my back, jumping long distances only to land comfortably with his mouth closed. But this time his eyes stretched wide with menace in a confrontational, focused glare.

I pointed to him and said, "Caleb, don't do this."

In a heartbeat, he bolted through the air, coming toward my throat, a target of attack, not play. I blocked, and he fell to the side along the fence. He sprang again. I blocked again. He sprang a third time, a fourth, a fifth, and then I lost track.

It became so dark I barely saw him. I felt myself tiring and knew I couldn't hold out much longer against the obsessed predator. Caleb never seemed to tire.

As I fought I called for help, first for Prayeri and then to God. In the midst of blocking the mountain lion's attacks, I saw a rippling effect in the air about seven feet to the right of me. In the rippling, I saw the image of a shadow, person-shaped, standing a couple of feet above the ground. It appeared to my mind's eye to be an angel, but he did nothing to help. He only watched.

Then a thought came to me, "Why isn't Caleb biting?" I had been attacked by a mountain lion once before, and she bit at each contact, screaming as she came. We now know that cougars attacking for defensive purposes bite anywhere on the victim. Cougars attacking offensively bite to kill, that is, on the throat or neck, and are completely silent throughout the entire assault. At the moment of my questioning, my guard went down.

Caleb banked off the hill next to me and latched onto the back of my neck with all four canines penetrating. I felt and heard the pop of my skin being punctured. I whirled around and pressed Caleb against the fence. He hung on my neck with his teeth deeply implanted.

I spun, and saw a being about eighteen inches off my right shoulder. He moved quickly away and up, about thirteen feet in the air and through an adjacent fence. The being swirled like the Van Gogh painting "The Starry Night." Within the swirl, I saw not one face but three.

They all looked at me but still did nothing to help.

I knew I could not hold Caleb by my neck for long and could not defend myself in that position. I dropped to the ground with the mountain lion still hanging on and tucked my head toward my chest. I lay partially on my side in an effort to pull away if an opportunity arose, but it didn't.

Unlike other large felines who just bite once and hold on, cougars chew, gaining more depth with each bite. I screamed in tortured pain. I had never experienced that much pain before despite numerous bites.

Since he held the back of my neck but could not break it, he moved forward toward my trachea to suffocate me. As he took a new position with his teeth, I again felt and heard his teeth penetrate. This time he punctured the top of my right lung. The wound later showed bubbles in the muscle, but his incision hadn't been large enough to collapse the lung.

As I lay there, I felt the process of dying, of my life draining. I knew how captured prey behaved, how they just resigned their lives, knowing their helpless condition. As they relax into the inevitable, rest brings a resurgence of energy. The prey gives a few final kicks and then dies. Many animals pretend to be dead already, hoping the predator will mistakenly release them. Occasionally, that hope is realized.

While being held, I cried out to God, "Lord, You're killing Your servant. Lord, You're killing Your servant."

From my awkward position, I saw the three-in-one being turn within itself and look away from me.

Then another being, traveling at a great speed, entered the atmosphere like a meteor, streaking from the south and turning east, directly toward me. As he slowed down, his appearance became more clear. He had an amorphous shape and was the size of several people. Grayish in color, he looked smoky with black "flames" around him, although he wasn't on fire. He stopped. Although I'd heard nothing, I knew he was told to halt.

While my life slipped away, the wolves howled in a nearby habitat. They were close enough to hear the commotion but couldn't see it. I knew they called Prayeri.

My escape had to be now. If Caleb moved forward again, he'd suffocate me. I called out to Prayeri one last time.

To my surprise and relief, I heard her scream, "Caleb!" She was still too far away to see me. Over a hundred yards away, she had three gates to get through, one of which she had locked. On her way, she picked up a plastic thirty-gallon drum and came running over the hills toward my voice.

When she approached me, Caleb released his hold, probably fearful of being hit with the drum. Prayeri set the drum down and helped me to my feet. My head fell against my right shoulder. I held it up with both hands and stumbled in a slouch toward the gate.

Prayeri's parents, T.J. and Mattie Powers, have a house close by, so we headed there. We knocked on the front door and went inside. I asked them to put towels down so I wouldn't bleed all over the carpeting. Shots of pain streaked through my neck and head, making it difficult to lie down. As I rolled on the floor in agony, I asked for a pain pill and Mattie provided two migraine tablets.

Prayeri called our park doctor, Bill McCabe, who met us at the hospital in about an hour. While Prayeri ran to recheck the gates to Caleb's new habitat and to get the van, I became overwhelmed with renewed appreciation for my wife. Love for her now poured through me in a way I had never known. When she returned, I told her what was happening to me. She looked astonished. She hadn't expected to hear about love at the moment. As we arrived at the hospital, the pain pills began to do their work, and I could discuss my injuries calmly.

The doctors seemed concerned about the punctured lung and the swollen arteries around my neck, which could have indicated a blood clot and a possible stroke. By 3:30 AM, the tests were complete—no blood clots, no collapsed lung. They rolled me back to the emergency room, where Prayeri waited.

I told her again about my new understanding of how much I loved her and of the encompassing strength of this love. I'd never experienced anything so profound. It was as if I finally appreciated all of her caring and support, the little and big things she'd done over the years to be one with me, and I wanted to do the same for her. I wanted to thank her for being the heart of my life.

I saw the effect it had on her. This enormous love magnified the way she felt about me, surrounding both of us. Love seemed to sparkle in the room, and that was only the beginning. It was a seed. I knew it was meant to grow tall, strong and beautiful. With nurturing, this love would enliven every moment we spent together and be plenty enough to share with others.

Ten days later, I had healed enough to be back in shows, although it would be months before I fully recovered.

Someone asked, as they frequently do, "What's the worst accident you've ever had?"

I told this story. I could see the positive effect it had on the audience. Some came back the following week and said the love in my story had touched their lives.

For the love that has grown out of this episode, the pain was an acceptable price to pay. I would do it again for Prayeri. This injury had meaning and purpose, and the outcome glows in my heart as a gift beyond price.

An incident like this cougar attack would normally be judged as bad. But though the experience was painful, retelling it has proven beneficial to many people. They've felt stronger love for their spouses, parents, friends and children, people they took for granted, and suddenly realized their relationships meant more than any other physical thing on earth. We often don't fully appreciate the people that are always there for us. In an instant they could be gone, and what a void would take their place. How important it is to show them your love while you can.

The incident also brings thoughts of those beings who appeared in the midst of that turmoil. Over the years, each time I have truly felt my life on the line I've observed everything in slow motion. I could see every detail of the animal attempting to do me harm. In each case, I experienced a heightened awareness. When the first being appeared, I became cognizant of the "veil," a term sometimes used to describe the barrier between the physical and the spiritual regions. It appeared like a curtain of water or "thick air," a definite barrier. The being hung in mid-air, poking through this veil, as if he wanted to help but was not allowed to because of a greater purpose that kept him from assisting me.

The three-in-one beings stayed remarkably close to me during the attack, almost in my space. Actually, we seemed to be sharing the same space, although we did not collide. The Three acted as one, although they appeared clearly as three. To me, they seemed to have invited the attack.

Just at the moment that I felt my spirit come out of my body through my head, I gave one last call for help—and Prayeri heard. My spirit swept back into its physical shell. I noticed that whether perceived from within my body or out of it, I remained me—feelings, thoughts, consciousness, everything!

The last being came for one purpose, to be my escort. The three-in-one stopped him, so he just looked on. Perhaps it is best to let each person make up his own mind who the players were in this drama. For me, it was obvious, even while the entire incident played out I had no doubt who any of the individuals were.

In anyone's life, traumatic situations such as this weigh heavily in measuring the value of one's existence. They bring the awareness that life is not simply composed of things or strivings but of relationships, both physical and spiritual.

THE PRISTINE INCIDENT

I glanced down at my watch. It read 12-02-91, 12:02 PM, Monday. I stood in front of the park as workmen installed two giant wrought iron gates. Suddenly, I received an urgent but garbled intuition. I detected a distress call, but it was unintelligible. These kinds of messages are not uncommon when one is close to animals. However, in this case, because the message seemed unclear, I dismissed it as just my own mind.

But the message returned again, even stronger. I knew I had to respond. The direction of distress focused plainly—southwest. I thought perhaps it concerned some of our reptiles, but that later proved to be just my idea. Immediately, I told the workmen, "Something's wrong. I have to go."

I ran by one of the habitats where I found Saginaw, Passage, Sahara, Saja and Eclipse staring in the same direction—southward. As I passed Java and Shanta, they, too, stared in that direction. Something was obviously wrong. It could have been a coyote or another local animal that somehow entered the rear of the park.

As I raced toward the ominous direction, I came on a horrible sight. Pristine, a young leopard, writhed at the chain link fence, her foreleg being stretched through the links, firmly grasped in the jaws of a lioness. Her right leg had been yanked up to the shoulder. It scraped and bulged against the heavy wire. The lioness' male companion stood protectively beside her, glaring at me as I approached.

"Drop her!" I yelled. To my surprise, the lioness immediately let go. The leopard was a major possession, and I'd never seen a lion give up such a possession on command only, either before or since.

Pristine pulled her front leg back through the fencing into the safety of her own habitat. I couldn't assess the leopard's condition from my vantage point. I needed to get to her as soon as possible. The quickest way in led me directly through the lion habitat. In I went, running cautiously. But about halfway through, the male lion began his defensive charge. I saw him coming. His attack speed seemed reduced to slow motion.

A charging lion is unmistakable. His intent is obvious. This one traveled at charging speed. His head had lowered to the level of his back, so I could see his shoulder blades rising and falling like pistons. His brow had furrowed and his eyes became slits. The air shook with his defensive roar, letting me know I had violated his possession and territory.

I called to him to stop, but he kept coming. His head lowered into position, to be used as a battering ram, with jaw to be flung wide at the last moment before impact. He had me, and I knew it.

Suddenly, something miraculous happened. Just as he positioned to overpower me, he appeared to hit a soft glass wall. He stopped, and looked at me. I stood there, staring at him. Impact had not come as I had expected.

I proceeded to the gate that led to Pristine's habitat. When I arrived, I found her sitting quite calmly, possibly in shock. Again I was surprised. She seemed extremely alert and aware of me. Though the injury to the leg had been severe, she had lost little blood. The pulling must have compressed the veins.

I told her, "I'm going to pick you up and take you to the hospital. Your injury isn't life-threatening. You'll be all right." I lifted the one-year-old wounded leopard and carried her against my chest through another, unoccupied habitat. Then I set her down in a double-entry enclosure, telling her, "I'll be right back."

I called the veterinary hospital and headed for the truck. When I returned, she remained docile as I picked her up again and put her into the camper of the pickup truck and locked her in.

She knew I was helping her. As we drove, she could see me through the cab window, and I could talk to her.

Twice I felt her ask me, "Are we there yet?"

And I responded, "We're almost there."

When we arrived, Dr. Irv Ingram and his staff had everything ready and waiting. We closely examined Pristine's leg. She had cleaned all the dirt and debris out of the entire wound. She looked at us as if anticipating our decision as to what would most help her.

The conclusion became obvious. Because most of the veins and nerves had been torn out, there would be no way to save the leg. we had to amputate. I sedated Pristine, and she quietly fell asleep. The nurses prepped her leg for the procedure. I scrubbed up to assist Irv. The operation itself was relatively simple. Soon Pristine had three legs.

Then we waited for her to partially wake up. After she roused, I drove her back to the park. When we arrived, I took her into our house, where she began to walk around. She wanted to use her missing leg, but realized nothing was there. Over and over she moved the muscles in the shoulder, but to no avail. She began to hop as if she had been doing it all her life. Then she slept deeply.

The next day, she woke ready to go. She began walking. She even ate—a good sign. We kept her in the house a couple of days, but she wanted out. She moved around with incredible ease; she even ran within a few days. Her speed increased remarkably and her balance improved.

Her life continued just as before. She still played with other cats—cougar, jaguar, and even a couple of tigers many times her size. To this day, she can easily knock down a two-hundred-pound male cougar, Chisum. She holds no grudge and seems to consider her condition a minor inconvenience.

Pristine did not lose her life or herself, and she's never seemed depressed about what might have been or shouldn't have happened. Instead, she has become an example of how to handle a disabling physical condition.

Pristine had been back on display only a few days when a woman visited the park who had recently had an arm amputated. She told one of our staff members that she had been afraid to go out in public for fear that people would stare at her. Finally, she had mustered enough courage to come to Out of Africa. That day, the woman met Pristine.

At the time, the physically challenged leopard lived near the entrance of the park. Information about her was posted on her habitat. The woman read Pristine's story and a poem by Randy Withrow, one of our annual members who later became a staff member. The leopard's story gave her renewed courage. She said, "If Pristine can do it, so can I."

Pristine is an ambassador helping those who are physically and mentally challenged. Her good, kind and sensitive nature has made her one of the most important members at Out of Africa. Many returning visitors ask where she is and are relieved to know she is doing well. Pristine's accident and recovery have been a source of encouragement to many people. She has devoted visitors who make a point to say hello to her whenever they come to the park. Often, she is up front where she can be easily seen and she enjoys the attention. Pristine's life is fulfilled. She paid a high price to be part of a plan for good that is greater than herself.

Now, as to what happened that day, when the male lion should have greatly injured or killed me—why am I still here? After many years of experience with exotic animals, I can think of no physical reason the lion didn't follow through on his instincts. He could not have stopped on his own; his speed was too great. Clearly, he intended to harm me, and I certainly did not present a threat big enough to deter his attack. To this day, he is the wildest and most assertive animal I have ever known. Other animals have difficulty controlling their instincts, but he doesn't even make an attempt to do so. His instincts simply control him. He lives for the relationship he has with his wife and is constantly concerned about her protection and well-being. He has not veered from this one objective since they married. I must conclude that the lion did not stop himself. An unseen force stopped him.

PRISTINE—THE PICTURE OF SACRIFICE, A TRUE HERO OF THE WILD.

CHAPTER EIGHT

Can You See Me?

Why are you looking at me like that?
    Are you sad?
        Do you pity me?

Do you mean to make me feel bad?
    You used to look in my eyes.
        Now you look at my empty shoulder.

Come here, I'll help you.
    You seem to need it.
        First, leave your pain behind.

What is it you think has changed?
    My leg is done, but my essence
        —did not live there.

Do you know how much I can lose?
    Before I lose myself?
        Much more than you must think.

If I told you sorrow and sadness
    —is not my need,
        would you understand?

If you focus you can see me as you did before.
    Can you see me?
        You don't have to look hard.

Can you see I'm not less than I was?
    I can even be more.
        Can you see?

No, I did not lose my spirit.
    Now, come run with me,
        and don't lose yours.

            —from a friend of Pristine

LESSONS FROM THE ANIMALS

In the process of gathering information on how animals think and respond to life, we find that we have actually gathered information on people as well. The animals act like mirrors, reflecting the composite of the people who watch them—less several uniquely human qualities, such as advanced consciousness and creativity, written language, mathematics, reliance on time, religion and idol worship, pride, greed, lust, lying, morality, intentionally decreasing awareness through drugs and alcohol, premeditated murder and suicide.

How do people compare with the best of the wild? Do we hold to certain principles, or do we just blow in the wind according to every whim that presents itself? If we as individuals utilized just the principles found in this book, would we change our decisions? Would we change our lives? Would those changes be for the better?

These principles have been field tested for eons for survival and quality of life. They are right more often than not, and being right can translate into success in any endeavor. But merely being right about a subject is not enough to satisfy life—animal or human.

In order for a life to be satisfied, one must accomplish a purpose greater than one's self. Self-seeking purposes are important but incomplete. I might achieve wealth and fame, but they are both means; they

WOULD YOU BE HIS FRIEND IF HE ASKED YOU? JAVA, A HUGE, MAGNIFICENT LION IN HIS PRIME, IS THE ANIMAL KING AT OUT OF AFRICA WILDLIFE PARK.

are not ends. They are highways to a commonly shared, good goal. It is the end result attained for the benefit of all that becomes an acceptable, complete life. Therefore, this should be life's goal—to align our path with a greater path that is in balanced, harmonious relationship with God, man and animals.

The first step is to recognize that man is not an accident. Each of us is important and essential to complete our part of the relay race. And we are never truly alone. Our efforts affect everyone and everything around us, in one degree or another. God has a master plan for Himself and a corresponding subordinate plan for us. He provides the sustenance for us to complete our race. God loves us, and His plan includes us all. If we rebel, purposing to do our own thing, how will we achieve anything worthwhile?

The second step is to recognize our own specific instincts that guide us to an orientation, our occupation in life. Happiness comes from doing what is good, that which is our appointed talent. If you don't know what your talent is, ask the Manufacturer. He made us specifically. We are His design.

Step three is to learn and apply the principles of survival to every aspect of our lives so we are strong in all areas. Learning is a process necessary for our own well-being. But learning comes in other ways than just intellectual processing through the five senses. The purest learning comes through discernment.

It is the mechanism animals use to alert themselves to something desired or not desired. Discernment is a silent language perceived in mental images and feelings that are translated into words. It knows no geographical limits or species boundaries but is designed to cross the space between living beings. It has a spiritual quality as old as life and as new as the latest creature born. It is a capacity to communicate.

Contained in this arena are both life and death. Discernment enhances choice and gives persuasion to one side or another. It is often the driving force behind greatness and the spiraling impetus to disaster. It often comes as an idea. Proper understanding of discernment is the essential ingredient for one to achieve his or her plan within The Plan. It can be our telephone to God—and His to us.

WALKING IN THE WILD

If you would like to experience contact with the wild side of nature, then I invite you to walk with me into a habitat with an adult Siberian tiger. Imagine, if you will, the clink of metal as I unlock the door to provide us entrance into another world, a world you may have dreamed of entering. You feel your heart rise to your throat and pound uncontrollably. You are light-headed, and you realize there is no turning back.

I usher you in first. Then I step in behind you, and you hear the click of the lock on the first gate. There is one more gate to go. I step in front of you and lift the latch. Your heart races even faster as you gaze into the habitat that stretches before you. The ground is dry and level, and the air smells of dust and animals. Two large acacia trees shade us, and you can hear the leaves rustle in the breeze that now cools your moist skin. A shadow of dire premonition sweeps over you, and you know you're vulnerable.

Lying among shrubs about a hundred feet away, a tiger watches you, assessing your every action.

Part of you screams in fear and wants to turn tail for the safety outside the fence. The other part says, "I hope it will be all right. Dean knows what he's doing. Besides, I'm already committed. I have to do it."

You step inside after me and I close the door. There is no quick way out.

"Come," I say. "Stay close. The tiger recognizes me, but he's not looking at me. He's staring at you!"

Before you didn't think animals had much expression and could not communicate their intent. You've just changed your mind. You take in every detail of the tiger. You watch the tiger's eyes, and look for the barest muscle twitch, wondering what the big predator is thinking.

The tiger stands and begins to walk toward us. His pace is deliberate. As he approaches, you note every movement, every step. He seems to be moving in slow motion.

You seem to be breathing in slow motion. The sound of your own breath roars like the blast of a hot-air balloon then seems to stop altogether as your entire attention focuses on the tiger.

He's approaching, his gaze intent on you. His eyes are larger than you expected and so is he! His paws are huge, and his head is bigger than your whole chest. He's enormous, and he seems to grow larger the closer he gets.

Somehow, six hundred pounds on the other side of the fence was smaller, a lot smaller. Six hundred pounds! That's the size of three heavyweight fighters. In one package, and with fangs and claws. And enough muscle to shred you like confetti.

HOLDING ON IS SOMETIMES MORE DIFFICULT THAN IT LOOKS. PARK VISITORS ENJOY CARRYING COLOSSUS, A HUGE BURMESE PYTHON.

BEFORE SPARRING IN THE MANNER IN WHICH TAJ, A WHITE BENGAL TIGER, AND JAMAICA, A BLACK LEOPARD (PANTHER), ARE DOING, IT IS NECESSARY THAT THEY BOTH HAVE PREVIOUSLY DECIDED TO BE FRIENDS.

This is it. The tiger is almost on top of us. He hasn't taken his eyes off you since you entered, as if you were a wary gazelle. You hear me say, "Good, Saginaw. This is my friend . . ."

Your own name you don't hear. Your mind is filled with this enormous cat, black stripes on burnt orange fur and a white chin ruff along those massive jaws. Your mind is in shock and your body refuses to move.

Just then he reaches for your leg with a paw that looks the size of a dinner plate. He easily pulls your foot off the ground, and you struggle to maintain balance. You've resigned yourself to losing a leg. You'd escape if you could.

He brings your leg to his mouth, and his four huge canines go around it. Your leg fits in his mouth like a toothpick. Your mind escapes, leaving your body in that instant to whatever condition the tiger chooses. You're in shock.

"Be good, Saginaw," I say.

The tiger sets your leg down. You don't know if he has bitten through you or not, but it hurts as if your shins had whacked into a table. Where his jaws grabbed you, your pants leg clings wetly to your skin.

Then you hear a voice, my voice. "It's okay, Saginaw. He's a friend. He loves tigers. Do you like him?"

Your mind is back in your body. The tiger is just standing in front of you. He's looking away. Someone else has caught his attention outside the habitat.

You breathe a sigh of relief—the first breath you can remember since the tiger approached. You don't believe you are hurt, but you don't dare check. Your eyes are fixed on the most impressive creature you have ever encountered. His hair is thick enough to lose a hand in. His shoulders are massive. His teeth are hidden, but you know they are hard and sharp enough to rip meat. His head is magnificent, and his eyes, so large, mesmerizing with inhuman intensity.

Some of your fear has left, and now you can think—not that it seems to matter at that moment. You are regaining your composure, and you are beginning to be yourself again. Your pride returns.

You ask, "Can I touch him?"

"For a moment," I reply. "Pet him. Now's your chance."

You see your hand reaching out almost as if it was on auto-remote. You feel the tiger's coarse hair and the firm muscles of his back. The

CHAPTER EIGHT

power and strength of his body feel like skin-sheathed rock. It is apparent that if he decided to kill you, you could do nothing.

Then you hear me say, "It's time. Thank you, Saginaw. See you later."

We begin to walk slowly backwards, never taking our eyes off the tiger. As we reach the gate, I open the latch and usher you inside the double entry. You release a great sigh. Then I unlock the outside gate, pushing it open for you. You walk through, but even outside you don't feel the ground. You're not floating, but you're not completely back to yourself.

You've done it! You've touched the tiger, and you're alive! You're still in shock and don't know whether you have been injured or not—but you don't care. "Thank you, thank you," you hear yourself say. "You don't know how much this means to me. I've dreamed about this all my life! Thank you."

"You're welcome," I answer. "You've entered the wild and lived. Your life was in his hands, and he didn't take it. You were at his mercy, and he allowed you to touch him. Remember what this means to you. Remember him and those like him. If they are to survive, it's up to you. You are now his friend. Learn of him and from him. Ask his Maker what you can do for him. His purpose was to tell you. Your purpose is to tell others. Union of spirit—God, human and animal is what we seek—oneness. It is within His design that He desires reunion.

Allow me to tell you about Him, the Maker who made the tiger. Let me dispel a few myths about Him, so we can have a clearer picture of Him and what He expects. He does not force His Will on you or take yours away. He is a gentleman and only guides you according to what He already knows is best for you in the long run.

He would like you to be in His symphony—"The Rock of Ages." He is like an orchestra leader who conducts many musicians to play melodically so the melody is music to His ears—and ours.

He doesn't change you overnight. It is a process like learning to type—the more you practice, the better you get. You don't have to go anywhere to receive His love. He is with you now. Anyone who says, "Jesus is Lord (boss) of my life" and seeks to fulfill this agreement through the principles of survival becomes a citizen of Heaven and has eternal life. Just believe that Jesus came, died for you and your mistakes and that He rose again. We know Jesus is God because He beat death. Act upon this belief and you belong to God. All you have ever done is forgiven. Now you must forgive those who have wronged you.

This is why forgiveness is so important. Unforgiveness in any form is the barrier to a relationship. If you decide to apply for citizenship in Heaven and truly mean it, you may also ask, in Jesus' Name, for a healing for whatever condition is affecting you—illness, injury, depression, loneliness, gluttony, bad habits, pride, greed, lust, lying, intentionally reducing awareness, blaming others, gossip, negative judgments of others, perversions, idol worship and bad attitude. Nothing is impossible for Him, but it usually takes us a little longer to work things out. Don't quit. He didn't quit on you; He died for you. Would you do that for Him? Keep your commitment because He keeps His. His Will is that you be in good health and that you live your life abundantly as you learn about Him and follow His ways.

By the way, if you are still having problems reconciling creation vs. evolution, dismiss it for now. Your life, fulfillment and destiny are more important than nameless opinions and bones. All that will be revealed to you at the right time. You are more important than a hundred fossils. You are alive; the fossils are not.

Pick up a copy of His book. It is the number one best seller ever. It was the first book printed. It goes under the name, The Bible. You may also wish to find some other people who believe like you do. Ask The

CHAPTER EIGHT

Lord to guide you so you can learn more about Him and how He deals with others like yourself. Keep in mind that what I am talking about is not religion; it is a relationship, a personal relationship with Our Father, His Son and The Holy Spirit. It is a spiritual and physical experience. It is a journey of great importance to you and Him. He wants you back! Go back where you came from. Repent. It means to return to the high point from which you have fallen. The entire Bible can be explained in two sentences—six words: "Live in Me," Genesis 1–2 and, "Return to Me," Genesis-Revelation.

If you are confused about the Trinity, consider Them as a team named The Lord (God). Our Father is the Captain, Jesus is the Quarter-back and The Holy Spirit plays the game. We are the score. The other team is called Evil, and Satan is its captain. Remember, in any scrimmage a lot of effort is needed to win. You will get hurt. You will need to apply yourself as if this is your last game. Ask Him for each play. Don't play it on your own.

If you are wondering if the Lord wants you, know that He has put the idea in your mind to ask the questions. Have You chosen me? Am I actually from You? You can know the answer is, "Yes," if you have always felt out of place. This is the universal sign, experience and feeling common to all those who are of God, no matter what present condition you are in right now. If you just never seem to fit, you belong to God. Make reservations for your return trip now. He is waiting. Then you will learn why we are here.

Our job on earth is simple. Walk with God and keep His principles. Teach others to do the same by loving our neighbors as ourselves. Care for the animals, plants and the earth. Subdue the enemy, the evil one. Return to the Lord with the fruit of victory.

Remember, according to His Book, which contains all the plays, He is coming soon! May the blessings of the Lord Jesus Christ be with you always, even unto the end of the Age. Come, Lord Jesus. Amen!

CHAPTER EIGHT

A Final Word

THE FORMULA TO LOVE GOD

As God's creation, we must revolve all our activity around Him. Trust Him. He as a being must become the center of our lives. Give your life to Him. Does your way really work? Are you as satisfied with your life as you could be?

Meet with Him daily. Write down in a log what He says and your responses and experiences. Be honest. Become pure in His eyes by listening and yielding to His ways so you can become like Him. He will remove confusion by providing guidance.

Decide to peel away personal characteristics and activities that He and you would be ashamed of if you were seen doing them together. Be sensitive and feel Him enjoy your day with you. Do not become distracted by too many activities. Be careful and budget your time within limits so He doesn't become second or forgotten in your life.

All activities, including projects He gives us, our occupations and social activities must always remain secondary. Our communion is first, which includes time just for Him.

He must always be our first love. This is an individual commitment, no matter who else is related to us—spouse, parents, children and friends.

Love the Lord first and most at all times, places and above all, for He is and has the answer to all questions, regardless of circumstances and emotions. He is greater than what we see and feel, think and predict. Know that He is with you and has already made arrangements in every situation.

Know the Lord, not just about Him. He has been lonely for His creation to love Him as He loves us. He has always been, and He has always been alone—forever. Who in all creation has ever filled the emptiness of His personal loneliness? Who has "married" Him, spirit to spirit, soul to soul, to see Him from His lonely hurt? This was the primary motivation to create us, to fill His broken heart.

Who wants to be alone forever? No one, not even God. All creatures ask and expect Him to fulfill them. Do we ask about Him? Do we pray for Him to be fulfilled? Who has truly communed with Him? To live with Him fully requires a couple, male and female, for that is why He created us man and woman. However, any two gathered in His name will work.

The marriage supper of the Lamb is an actual marriage of Himself, the Bridegroom, and His creation, the Bride. We must choose Him through our free will. He is our "lover" and we are to pursue Him and to fulfill His otherwise broken heart. We must continue our honeymoon forever or His heart will break again.

This is the sole purpose of our soul, the reason why He created living beings with free will. We are intended to commune with Him forever.

To love the Lord as He loves us is a creative act of love by His creation. By communing with Him, we live in Him and He in us. Our future is changed. He is no longer our maintenance man to pick up after us. He is our Husband, the Architect, the Builder, the Provider, the Protector, the Lover inspired by His bride, who truly loves Him and is concerned about His wellbeing, His desires and needs. We become His inspiration, not His perspiration.

Now we can love Him for Himself, not what we can get from Him. We are now one.

Do not ask only what He can do for us but what we can be for Him. Love Him first and most forever.

If we do this, we'll never know fear again and we will never be alone. Perfect love removes fear. Love the Lord and fulfill Him. Then He will love and fulfill us without measure forever. Do it all in Jesus' name. Remember, a relationship with God doesn't come all at once. It takes time to develop. You are important to yourself and to Him, so it's worth the effort. He believes in you. Believe in Him.

Epilogue

In June 2004 we relocated the park with all the animals to Camp Verde, Arizona, a small town about a hundred miles north of Phoenix off Interstate 17. The relocation was necessary because a new tribal council denied us additional land to accommodate new animals, many of them rescues.

So we searched for a new home in a cooler climate, which we found in the foothills of the Mingus Mountains, surrounded by the Prescott National Forest.

With help of over 1,400 volunteers and many answered prayers, we tore down the old facility while erecting temporary enclosures at the new site. Then we built natural spacious habitants for the animals according to their needs.

One year later on Memorial Day Weekend the new Out of Africa Wildlife Park reopened as a 104-acre natural sanctuary with plenty of room for many animals and visitors.